Great British Puddings

Great British Puddings

Mary and Debbie Smith

FOREWORD BY

DERRICK COOPER

AFTERWORD BY

GODFREY SMITH

To Amanda and Candy

First published in Great Britain in 1996 by
PAVILION BOOKS LIMITED
26 Upper Ground, London SE1 9PD

Designed by Andrew Barron and Collis Clements Associates

A CIP catalogue record for this book is available from the British Library

ISBN 1 85793 893 3 (hardback)
ISBN 1 85793 902 6 (paperback)

Typeset in Foundry Wilson
Printed and bound by BPC Consumer Books Ltd, Aylesbury

2 4 6 8 10 9 7 5 3 1

This book may be ordered by post direct from the publisher.
Please contact the Marketing Department.
But try your bookshop first.

CONTENTS

FOREWORD

It is perhaps typical of our offhand attitude to eating that we should have bestowed a term of abuse on the very delights that define our native gastronomy. You can hear the derision in the voice when people call out 'pudding face' or 'pudding head'. Remember Falstaff mocked as the ox with the pudding in his belly? And that's strange, because pudding is the dish we have always done better than anyone else. In the old days when food still had a regional taste, towns from Canterbury, Cheltenham and Chester to Tadcaster, Tiverton and Tunbridge put themselves on the culinary map with the eponymous puddings. The gudewives *of Nottingham had their buttery batter and apple pudding; in Chester they were famous for a custard pudding bolstered with breadcrumbs; Ipswich cooks put almonds in their oven-baked puddings, and the Exeter folk used ratafia and raisins.*

But there is more to what Burns memorably called the 'pudding race' than the merely substantial. Plum pudding, suet pudding and bread pudding have a weighty place at the end of the meal, but, as Mary and Debbie Smith demonstrate so simply in the pages that follow, there is froth and lightness in abundance: jellies, junkets, pies, tarts, fools, custards, ice creams, sorbets and much more. There's a pernicious urban myth particularly attractive to people determined to stay officiously alive for ever that the pudding is nutritionally incorrect – nice, yes, but excessively naughty. But puddings are not about calories and cholesterol, they are about enjoyment and pleasure. If Brillat-Savarin's last words really were, 'Bring on the dessert, I think I am about to die,' how right he was.

What is pleasing abut this mouthwatering book is that it places the glories of puddings in a social and historical context. All the old favourites are here, and all manner of rare delights: Poached Vanilla Cherries with Fresh Mint, Quince Blancmange and Tea Sorbet with Rum, to name but three.

This enthusiastic celebration of sweet things steamed, simmered, poached, baked and chilled restores the pudding to its rightful place:

'tis the dessert that graces all the feast
For an ill end disparages the rest.

Derek Cooper, 1996

INTRODUCTION

The British pudding is back. In the past, puddings were a staple filler for the poor or a sophisticated delight for the rich. Then, after the Second World War, dieting became a national sport and puddings went out of fashion. We have now emerged into a new world in which the immense cornucopia of British puddings is being rediscovered, celebrated and enjoyed.

Now, though, the pud is seen firmly in its modern context: served in its starring role, as one of the principal delights of British cooking. Our new wave of young brilliant chefs are exploiting and reinventing our forgotten heritage from day to day. A pudding, in short, has now become not so much a guilty British treat as a heady British triumph.

The deeper we dig into our old cookery books the more forgotten treasures come to light. The names our forefathers gave to our puddings are endlessly rich in their variety and eccentricity. They range from the grand old staples like Trifles and Crumbles to Spotted Dick or Apricot Fool. Honest perennials, such as Summer Pudding and Treacle Tart, are now being offset by exotic rediscoveries like Sussex Pond Pudding and Shakespeare's Iced Pudding.

We have used the word pudding to cover the whole range of sweet dishes, because every other term we considered has weird resonances. Words like dessert, sweet or afters are far more accurate, but each rings the wrong bell: dessert is too foreign, sweet is too plonky and afters too jokey. So puddings it shall be.

Appreciating the British pudding is nothing new. When Francois Misson came here just 300 years ago his admiration in *Memoires et Observations faites par un voyageur en Angleterre* was unstinted: 'They bake them in an oven, they boil them 50 several ways: BLESSED BE HE THAT INVENTED PUDDING, for it is a manna that hits the palates of all sorts of people'.

CHAPTER 1

PIES, PASTRY AND CRUMBLES

Apple Dumplings
Apple or Blackberry and Apple Pie
Apple Turnovers
Apricot or Plum Pie
Mincemeat Plate Pie
Cherry, Raspberry or Blackberry Plate Pie
Star Mince Pies
Lemon Meringue Pie
Pumpkin Pie
Apricot and Almond Crumble
Blackberry, Apple and Hazelnut Crumble
Raspberry and Banana Oat Crumble
Rhubarb and Walnut Crumble

Our deep-dish fruit pie is one of the principal glories of British cooking and so unusual that it still amazes visitors from abroad. Essentially it must be made in an ovenproof dish with a wide rim, so that a light and crisp buttery pastry forms a sealed dome over the fruit. We associate these pies with lazy family Sunday lunches – their fillings changing with the season – as a perfect partner to the traditional roast with all its trimmings.

There does not seem to be any logical explanation for the name pie or tart. Our celebrated Lemon Meringue Pie with its clouds of gleaming white meringue over a luscious lemon curd in a pastry case is really a tart, whereas Pear Tart is a shallow double-crusted plate pie.

Crumbles are a delicious variation on deep fruit pies, perhaps even more appealing because the crumble, sprinkled over the fruit, absorbs some of the fruit juices, but stays crisp on top. Crumbles are extremely easy to make, are virtually infallible and are good to serve to a large number of people.

APPLE DUMPLINGS

'Coleridge holds that a man cannot have a pure mind who refuses apple dumplings. I am not sure but he is right' (Charles Lamb).

Cox's Orange Pippins are ideal for this recipe. We tried various different ways of enclosing the apples in the pastry, but found this method, where the apple is left open at the top, to be the best.

SERVES 8
use a baking sheet

For the pastry

450g/1lb plain white flour
225g/8oz butter, chilled and cut into pieces, plus a little extra for greasing
2 large eggs, beaten

For the apples

8 medium apples, peeled and cored
50g/2oz candied orange rind, finely chopped
50g/2oz caster sugar, plus a little extra for sprinkling
a little cold milk for brushing

Make the pastry as described on pages 181–2, wrap in greaseproof paper and leave to rest in the fridge for 30 minutes.

Preheat the oven to 200°C/400°F/Gas Mark 6 and butter the baking sheet.

Divide the pastry into 8 pieces and roll each piece into a circle about 20cm/8in in diameter. Place an apple in the centre of each piece of pastry, then fill the centre of each apple with the candied orange rind and sugar. Cut out 4 triangles of pastry (see diagram overleaf) to a depth about halfway between the apple and the pastry edge. Brush all the edges with milk, fold the pastry up around the apple, then press the edges together to seal them, leaving the top of the dumplings open. Trim off any excess pastry with a pair of kitchen scissors to make neat seams. Prick the pastry several times with a fork, brush the pastry all over with a little milk, then sprinkle with the extra sugar.

Arrange the dumplings on the prepared baking sheet. Bake for 20 minutes, then reduce the oven temperature to 170°C/325°F/Gas Mark 3 and bake for a further 15 minutes, testing that the apples are cooked with a skewer.

Serve immediately with cream, Custard Sauce (see page 173), Vanilla Ice Cream (see page 148) or natural yogurt.

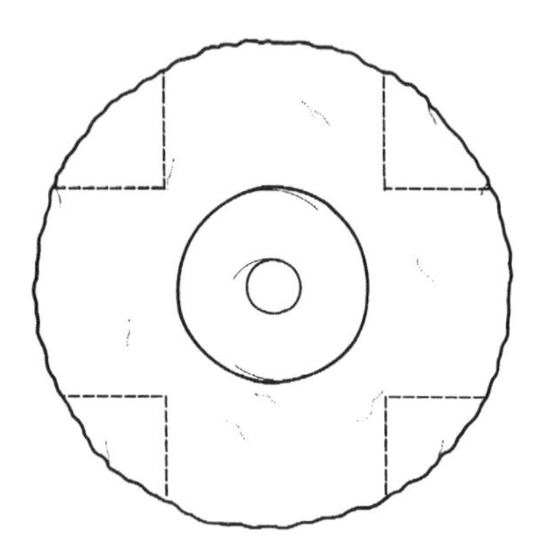

APPLE OR BLACKBERRY AND APPLE PIE

This is a traditional apple pie, the archetypal British dish which is much envied across the world, but all too often poorly imitated.

Florence White, in *Good Things in England* first published in 1932, quotes Abraham Hayward, QC, writing in *The Art of Dining* in 1852: 'The late Lord Dudley could not dine comfortably without an apple pie, as he insisted on calling it, contending that the term tart only applied to open pastry. Dining when Foreign Secretary, at a grand dinner at Prince Esterhazy's, he was terribly put out on finding that his favourite delicacy was wanting, and kept on murmuring pretty audibly, in his absent way: "God bless my soul! No apple pie." '

The following recipe has melting layers of apple slices, flavoured with lemon, under a crisp pastry crust. It is usually made in an oval pie dish with a flat rim.

The egg white and sugar glaze is from Mrs Beeton and can be replaced by a little cold milk brushed over the pastry before it is baked, with some caster sugar sprinkled on top.

SERVES 6–8
use a 2.4 litre/4 pint pie dish

For the pastry

275g/10oz plain white flour
150g/5oz butter, chilled and cut into pieces
1 medium egg
a little cold milk for brushing

For the filling

1.4kg/3lb cooking apples, peeled, cored and sliced
175g/6oz caster sugar
finely grated rind of ½ lemon
8 tbsp water

For the glaze

1 small egg white
about 15g/½oz caster sugar.

Make the pastry as described on pages 181–2, wrap in greaseproof paper, then leave it in the fridge to rest for about 30 minutes.

Preheat the oven to 200°C/400°F/Gas Mark 6.

Layer the apple slices into the pie dish, sprinkling the sugar in between the layers. Sprinkle over the lemon rind and water.

Roll out the pastry on a lightly floured surface into an oval shape slightly larger than the top of the pie dish, then cut a strip of pastry, about 2cm/¾in wide, from the outer edge. Brush the rim of the dish with a little milk and press the pastry strip onto it. Brush the pastry strip with a little more milk. Cover the whole pie with the remaining pastry and trim off any excess. Press the rim firmly to seal. Use the blunt edge of a knife to make a series of shallow indentations around the edge of the pastry. To scallop, press your thumb around the rim, and at the same time make shallow cuts in between each thumb print. With the point of a knife, make a number of slits in the pastry lid, then decorate with pastry leaves cut from the trimmings, sticking them in place with a little milk.

Bake the pie for 30 minutes. To glaze the pie, beat the egg white with a fork until it is frothy and brush it over the pastry. Sprinkle over the sugar and bake the pie for another 15 minutes until the pastry is a pale golden brown. Cover the pastry loosely with a piece of foil if it is getting too brown.

Serve warm or cold with cream, Custard Sauce (see page 173), Vanilla Ice Cream (see page 148) or natural yogurt.

VARIATIONS

A Blackberry and Apple Pie is made in exactly the same way by substituting 225g–450g/½lb–1lb blackberries for the same weight of apples.

Apple Turnovers

Apple Turnovers are at their best eaten as soon as possible after baking.

MAKES ABOUT 20 TURNOVERS TO SERVE 8–10
use 2 baking sheets

675g/1 ½lb cooking apples, peeled, cored and cut into pieces
15g/½oz butter, plus a little extra for greasing
1 tbsp lemon juice
grated rind of ½ lemon
50g/2oz light muscovado sugar
½ tsp ground cinnamon
250g/9oz puff pastry (see page 182)
1 small egg, beaten
demerara sugar for sprinkling

Place the apples, butter, lemon juice and rind in a large heavy-based saucepan and cook over a very low heat, stirring from time to time, until the apples are just tender. Add the sugar and ground cinnamon. Remove the lemon rind, purée the apples and leave to cool. Lightly butter the baking sheets.

Roll out the pastry on a lightly floured board to about 3mm/⅛in thick. Using a 7.5cm/3in pastry cutter, cut out about 20 pastry circles. Roll out each circle again lightly. Holding a circle of pastry in the flat of your hand, put a generous teaspoonful of apple purée in the middle of the pastry. Brush half the edge of the circle with beaten egg, fold the turnover in half and pinch the rim together well to seal. Return the turnover to the floured surface and mark the sealed edge with the back of a fork. Supporting the spine of the turnover with your thumb, make a few holes in the top of the pastry with a fork. Make the rest of the turnovers in the same way, place on the prepared baking sheet and leave to rest in the fridge for about 30 minutes. Preheat the oven to 200°C/400°F/Gas Mark 6.

Brush the turnovers with the rest of the beaten egg, then sprinkle with demerara sugar and bake for 15 minutes until golden brown.

Serve hot, warm or cold with cream, Custard Sauce (see page 173), Vanilla Ice Cream (see page 148) or natural yogurt.

Apricot or Plum Pie

This is a deep apricot pie which is covered in crisp pastry and is traditionally made in an oval pie dish with a flat rim.

SERVES 4–6
use a 1.5 litre/2½ pint pie dish

For the pastry

225g/8oz plain white flour
100g/4oz butter, chilled and cut into pieces
1 medium egg
a little cold milk for brushing
a little caster sugar for sprinkling

For the filling

900g/2lb apricots, halved and stoned
100g/4oz caster sugar
4 tbsp water

Make the pastry as described on pages 181–2, wrap in greaseproof paper and leave to rest in the fridge for 30 minutes.

Preheat the oven to 200°C/400°F/Gas Mark 6.

Pile the apricots into the dish and sprinkle over the sugar and water.

Roll out the pastry on a lightly floured surface into an oval shape slightly larger than the top of the pie dish then cut a strip of pastry, about 2cm/¾in wide, from the outer edge. Brush the rim of the dish with a little milk and press the pastry strip onto the rim. Brush the pastry strip with milk. Cover the whole pie with the remaining pastry and trim off the excess. Press the rim firmly to seal. Use the blunt edge of a knife to make a series of shallow indentations around the edge of the pastry. To scallop, press your thumb around the rim, and at the same time make shallow cuts in between each thumb print.

With the point of a knife, make a number of slits in the pastry lid, then decorate with pastry leaves, sticking them in place with a little milk.

Brush the complete pastry surface with milk, then sprinkle sugar on top.

Bake the pie for 30–40 minutes until the pastry is pale golden brown, covering it loosely with a piece of foil if it gets too brown.

Serve warm or cold, with cream, Custard Sauce (see page 173), Vanilla Ice Cream (see page 148) or natural yogurt.

VARIATIONS

Plums can be used in exactly the same way as the apricots.

Mincemeat Plate Pie

This plate pie is very easy to make at the same time as some Star Mince Pies (see page 00) and very useful to have in the freezer for unexpected guests.

SERVES 4–6
use a 23cm/9in pie plate (see page 179)

225g/8oz plain white flour
100g/4oz butter, chilled and cut into pieces
1 medium egg
450g/1lb Christmas Plum Mincemeat (see page 160)
a little cold milk for brushing
a little caster sugar for sprinkling

Make the pastry with the flour, butter and egg as described on pages 181–2, wrap in greaseproof paper and leave to rest in the fridge for 30 minutes.

Preheat the oven to 200°C/400°F/Gas Mark 6.

Roll out just over half the pastry on a lightly floured surface and line the pie plate. Spread the mincemeat over the pastry base. Roll out the rest of the pastry and cut into strips about 2cm/¾in wide. Arrange the strips over the mincemeat in a lattice pattern. Brush the ends of the strips with a little milk and press them into rim of the pastry base. Brush a little milk over the strips, sprinkle over some caster sugar and bake the pie for 25 minutes. Serve warm or cold, with cream, Custard Sauce (see page 173), Vanilla Ice Cream (see page 148) or natural yogurt.

Cherry, Raspberry or Blackcurrant Plate Pie

An appealing, old British way of cooking and preserving summer fruit, mentioned by Florio in 1598 as a 'pye plate'.

SERVES 4–6
use a 23cm/9in pie plate (see page 179)

For the pastry

225g/8oz plain white flour
100g/4oz butter, chilled and cut into pieces
1 medium egg
a little cold milk for brushing
a little caster sugar for sprinkling

For the filling

50g/2oz caster sugar
450g/1lb cherries, stalks removed and stoned

Make the pastry as described on pages 181–2, wrap in greaseproof paper and leave in the fridge to rest for 30 minutes.

Preheat the oven to 200°C/400°F/Gas Mark 6.

Roll out just under half the pastry on a lightly floured surface and line the pie plate. For the filling, sprinkle half the sugar over the pastry, arrange the cherries on top, then sprinkle on the rest of the sugar.

Roll out the rest of the pastry to a circle that is slightly larger than the pie plate. Brush the rim of the pastry in the plate with a little milk and place the pastry lid over the fruit. To seal the edges together well, press even thumb prints around the rim or make marks with the prongs of a fork. Make several slits in the pastry lid with the point of a knife, then brush the surface with milk, sprinkle over a little sugar and bake the pie for 25 minutes until the pastry is pale golden brown.

Serve warm or cold, with cream, Custard Sauce (see page 173), Vanilla Ice Cream (see page 148) or natural yogurt.

VARIATIONS

For Raspberry Plate Pie use 350g/12oz raspberries and 75g/3oz sugar. For Blackcurrant Plate Pie use 350g/12oz blackcurrants and 100g/4oz sugar. Or use a mixture of all three fruits.

Star Mince Pies

Because the mincemeat used in this recipe has a lot of juice, we found that the best way to make individual mince pies with it was to use a pastry star for the lid. This also makes the mince pies look particularly attractive, festive *and* unusual. The pies can be made in advance, stored in an airtight tin and eaten cold or warmed in the oven.

MAKES ABOUT 15 PIES
use 2 patty tins

225g/8oz plain white flour
100g/4oz butter, chilled and cut into pieces
1 medium egg
450g/1lb Christmas Plum Mincemeat (see page 160)
a little cold milk for brushing
caster sugar for sprinkling

Make the pastry with the flour, butter and egg as described on pages 181–2, wrap in greaseproof paper and leave to rest in the fridge for 30 minutes.

Preheat the oven to 200°C/400°F/Gas Mark 6.

Roll out the pastry on a lightly floured surface and cut out 15 circles with a 7cm/2¾in pastry cutter and 15 stars with a 6.5cm/2½in star cutter. Line the patty tins with the circles of pastry and fill each one with a heaped teaspoonful of mincemeat. Brush one surface of each pastry star with a little milk and place the stars, brushed side up, on top of the mincemeat. Sprinkle the pies with a little caster sugar.

Bake the pies for 15–20 minutes until pale golden, then cool on a wire rack.

Serve with Brandy or Rum Butter (see page 171) or cream.

LEMON MERINGUE PIE

This is a classic British pudding made with real lemon curd. It is a brilliant mixture of white foaming meringue contrasting with but complementing the richness of the curd and the tang of lemon. It was on the menu when Mary was taken out to lunch to meet her mother-in-law for the first time. She made it quite clear that Mary would have to learn how to make Godfrey's favourite pudding.

SERVES 6
use a 23cm/9in loose-based tart tin (see page 180)

For the pastry

175g/6oz plain white flour
75g/3oz butter
1 small egg

For the filling

3 medium eggs, beaten
225g/8oz caster sugar
100g/4oz butter, cut into pieces
finely grated rind of 3 large lemons
175ml/6fl oz lemon juice

For the meringue

3 large egg whites
100g/4oz caster sugar

Make the pastry and line the tart tin as described on pages 181–2, prick the base with a fork, then leave to rest in the fridge for 30 minutes.

Preheat the oven to 200°C/400°F/Gas Mark 6.

Bake the pastry blind (see page 182) for 10 minutes, then remove the greaseproof paper and beans and bake for a further 5 minutes.

Meanwhile, make the filling. Put the eggs, sugar, butter, lemon rind and juice into the top of a double boiler or in a heatproof bowl over simmering water. Stir continuously with a wooden spoon until the mixture has thickened, then pour into the pastry case.

Lower the oven temperature to 150°C/300°F/Gas Mark 2.

To make the meringue, whisk the egg whites until they are stiff, but not dry, then whisk in about half the sugar. Fold in the rest of the sugar with a metal spoon. Pile the meringue over the lemon filling, sealing it to the pastry edge, then bake for a further 30 minutes until the top is golden.

Serve warm or cold, with cream.

Pumpkin Pie

Although pumpkins have been largely replaced by marrows in Britain, they now seem to be having somewhat of a revival. We tend to associate Pumpkin Pie with Thanksgiving in America, but the original recipes are said to have been taken to the States by the Pilgrim Fathers. The American version is usually made with a spiced pumpkin purée.

This lovely autumnal recipe uses a mixture of finely chopped pumpkin and apple, flavoured with currants, candied rind and spice. It has been adapted from one in *Good Things in England* by Florence White, first published in 1932.

SERVES 6
use a 23cm/9in pie plate (see page 179)

For the pastry

225g/8oz plain white flour
100g/4oz butter, chilled and cut into pieces
1 medium egg
a little cold milk for brushing
caster sugar for sprinkling

For the filling

225g/8oz pumpkin flesh, finely chopped
225g/8oz apple, finely chopped
100g/4oz currants
50g/2oz mixed candied peel, finely chopped
75g/3oz caster sugar
1 tsp mixed ground spice
finely grated rind of ½ lemon

Make the pastry as described on pages 181–2, wrap in greaseproof paper and leave in the fridge to rest for 30 minutes.

Preheat the oven to 200°C/400°F/Gas Mark 6.

Roll out just under half of the pastry on a lightly floured surface and line the pie plate.

Mix together the filling ingredients and heap them onto the lined plate. Roll out the rest of the pastry, brush the rim of the pastry on the plate with milk, cover the pie with the pastry lid and press the edge well to seal. Make even thumb prints around the pastry rim or make shallow indentations with the back of a fork. Cut several slits in the lid with the point of a knife.

Brush the top of the pie with milk, then sprinkle with caster sugar and bake for 25 minutes until golden.

Serve warm, with cream, Custard Sauce (see page 173), Vanilla Ice Cream (see page 148) or natural yogurt.

Apricot and Almond Crumble

This lovely summer crumble is made with a combination of fresh apricots and ratafia biscuits.

SERVES 6–8
use a 2.4 litre/4 pint ovenproof dish

For the fruit

900g/2lb apricots, halved and stones removed
75g/3oz caster sugar
75g/3oz ratafia biscuits (see page 179), roughly chopped

For the crumble

225g/8oz plain white flour
100g/4oz butter, chilled and cut into pieces
75g/3oz caster sugar
25g/1oz flaked almonds

Preheat the oven to 180°C/350°F/Gas Mark 4.

Mix the apricots and sugar together gently in the ovenproof dish, then level out the fruit and sprinkle the ratafia biscuits on top.

To make the crumble, put the flour, butter and sugar into a food processor and process briefly until the mixture is crumbly. Alternatively, rub the butter into the flour until crumbly, then stir in the sugar.

Sprinkle the crumble mixture over the fruit, smooth the surface and scatter the almonds on top. Bake the crumble for about 55 minutes until the top is golden brown and the fruit is cooked.

Serve warm or cold, with cream, Custard Sauce (see page 173), Vanilla Ice Cream (see page 148) or natural yogurt.

Blackberry, Apple and Hazelnut Crumble

A classic combination of blackberry and apple with an unusual hazelnut crumble.

SERVES 4–6
use a 2.4 litre/4 pint ovenproof dish

For the fruit

450g/1lb cooking apples, peeled, cored and sliced
225g/8oz blackberries
100g/4oz caster sugar
3 tbsp cold water

For the crumble

175g/6oz plain white flour
100g/4oz butter, chilled and cut into pieces
75g/3oz demerara sugar
75g/3oz hazelnuts, toasted (see page 180) and chopped

Preheat the oven to 180°C/350°F/Gas Mark 4.

Mix the apples, blackberries and sugar together gently in the ovenproof dish. Add the water, then level out the fruit.

To make the crumble, put the flour and butter into a food processor and process briefly until the mixture is crumbly. Alternatively, rub the butter into the flour until crumbly. Stir the sugar and the hazelnuts into the crumble mixture, then spread evenly over the fruit. Bake the crumble for about 40 minutes until the crumble is golden brown and the fruit is cooked.

Serve warm, with cream, Custard Sauce (see page 173), Vanilla Ice Cream (see page 148) or natural yogurt.

VARIATION

This dish can be made with just apples, in which case increase the amount to 675g/1½lb.

Raspberry and Banana Oat Crumble

Crumbles are usually associated with autumn and winter. However, this combination of raspberries and bananas is very summery and delicate.

SERVES 6
use a 2.4 litre/4 pint ovenproof dish

For the fruit

450g/1lb raspberries
75g/3oz caster sugar
2 large ripe bananas, peeled and thinly sliced

For the crumble

100g/4oz plain white flour
100g/4oz porridge oats
100g/4oz butter, chilled and cut into pieces
75g/3oz demerara sugar

Preheat the oven to 200°C/400°F/Gas Mark 6.

Put the raspberries into the dish and sprinkle over the caster sugar. Level the fruit out gently, then arrange a layer of banana slices on top.

To make the crumble, put the flour, porridge oats, butter and sugar into a food processor and process in short bursts until the mixture resembles coarse breadcrumbs, but the oats have not disintegrated. Alternatively, mix together the flour and porridge oats, rub in the butter until the mixture resembles coarse breadcrumbs, then stir in the sugar.

Spread the crumble mixture evenly over the fruit and bake for 45 minutes until the top is golden brown.

Serve warm or cold, with cream, Custard Sauce (see page 173), Vanilla Ice Cream (see page 148) or natural yogurt.

Rhubarb and Walnut Crumble

The flavour of orange and walnuts make this crumble particularly delicious, but if you would prefer a plain crumble, use 225g/8oz flour instead of 175g/6oz. If the rhubarb is rather thick, cut it in half lengthways. Test that the rhubarb is cooked with a skewer.

SERVES 6–8
use a a 2.4 litre/4 pint ovenproof dish

For the fruit

900g/2lb rhubarb, trimmed and cut into 2.5cm/1in lengths
finely grated rind of 1 large orange
75g/3oz light muscovado sugar
50g/2oz sultanas

For the crumble

175g/6oz plain white flour
100g/4oz butter, chilled and cut into pieces
75g/3oz demerara sugar
75g/3oz walnuts, chopped

Preheat the oven to 180°C/350°F/Gas Mark 4.

Put the pieces of rhubarb into the dish, then mix in the orange rind and the sugar. Level out the fruit and sprinkle the sultanas over the top.

To make the crumble, put the flour, butter and sugar into a food processor and process briefly until the mixture is crumbly, then stir in the walnuts. Alternatively, rub the butter into the flour until crumbly, then stir in the sugar and the walnuts.

Sprinkle the crumble mixture evenly over the fruit and bake for 40 minutes until the top is golden brown and the rhubarb is cooked.

Serve warm with cream, Custard Sauce (see page 173), Vanilla Ice Cream (see page 148) or natural yogurt.

CHAPTER 2

TARTS

Apple Amber
Apricot Tart
Apple Cheesecake
Bakewell Tart with Fresh Raspberries
Chocolate Tart
Currant Curd Cheesecake
Custard Tart
Jam Tart with Almond Pastry Lattice
Lemon Cheesecake or Lemon Curd Tart
Parsnip and Ginger Flan
Pear Tart
Prune and Apple Tart with Brandy
Treacle Tart

LYLE'S GOLDEN
ABRAM LYLE & SONS
SUGAR REFINERS
454 g e

Before metal or earthenware dishes came into general use, meat, fish, fruit and custard were poured into pre-cooked pastry cases. The cases were called coffins, coffers or boxes of pastry – unprepossessing names which were soon simplified by the British to one all-embracing word for a particular British delight, the tart.

Treacle Tart is probably the greatest of them all and was for a long time considered simple staple fare. It has recently had a most remarkable revival and is back in vogue, served in the most fashionable British restaurants.

Unlike the French, we tend to fill our tarts with fruit purées and curds, rather than whole pieces of fruit which we put into puddings and pies.

Apple Amber

This melt-in-the-mouth tart consists of a rich pastry case filled with lightly spiced apple purée and covered in meringue.

SERVES 6

use a 23cm/9in loose-based tart tin (see page 180)

For the pastry

175g/6oz plain white flour
100g/4oz butter
50g/2oz caster sugar
1 small egg yolk
finely grated rind of ½ lemon

For the filling

675g/1½lb cooking apples, peeled, cored and cut into pieces
4 whole cloves
50g/2oz butter
3 generous tbsp honey
3 large egg yolks, lightly beaten

For the meringue

3 large egg whites
100g/4oz caster sugar

Make the pastry and line the tart tin as described on pages 181–2. Prick the base with a fork, then leave in the fridge to rest for 30 minutes.

Preheat the oven to 190°C/375°F/Gas Mark 5.

To make the filling, put the apples, cloves, butter and honey into a saucepan and cook gently over a low heat until the apples are just tender. Remove the cloves, purée the mixture and leave to cool a little. Mix the egg yolks in well, then pour the mixture into the pastry case and bake for 30 minutes.

Reduce the oven temperature to 150°C/300°F/Gas Mark 2.

To make the meringue, whisk the egg whites until they are stiff, but not dry, then whisk in about half the sugar. Fold in the rest of the sugar with a metal spoon. Pile the meringue over the apple filling, sealing it to the pastry edge, then bake for another 30 minutes until the top is golden.

Serve warm or cold, with cream, Custard Sauce (see page 73), Vanilla Ice Cream (see page 148) or natural yogurt.

Apricot Tart

This very traditional recipe is based on one in *Good Things in England* by Florence White (1932), who claims that it comes from *Adam's Luxury and Eve's Cookery* (1744) and originally from a *Proper Newe Booke of Cookerye* (1545).

This is not really how we expect a fruit tart to be, but is more like a heavenly apricot soufflé with a light creamy centre in a puff pastry crust. It is best eaten as soon as possible – certainly on the day it is made.

We made this tart with ready-made puff pastry and baked it blind in a circotherm electric oven at its hottest setting, which is equivalent to 250°C/475°F/Gas Mark 9. The pastry packet suggests cooking the pastry at 200°C/400°F/Gas Mark 6 or 220°C/425°F/Gas Mark 7 and the heat at which it should be baked probably depends on your oven, although it seems to be a case of the hotter the better. The base of the pastry will rise a little when the beans are removed, but will flatten again when the filling is added.

SERVES 6

use 23cm/9in loose-based tart tin (see page 180)

250g/9oz puff pastry (see page 181)
450g/1lb fresh apricots
100g/4oz caster sugar
4 medium egg yolks, lightly beaten
150ml/¼ pint double cream
2 medium egg whites

Roll the pastry out on a lightly floured surface to about 3mm/⅛in thick and line the tin. Leave the pastry sticking up a good 5mm/¼in above the rim of the tin and trim with a pair of kitchen scissors. Chill the lined tart tin for 30 minutes.

Preheat the oven to 250°C/475°F/Gas Mark 9 (see above).

Steam the whole apricots, covered, in a vegetable steamer or metal colander over simmering water until they are just tender, then remove the stones. Purée the apricots, then leave to cool slightly.

Bake the tart blind (see page 182) for 10 minutes, then remove the the greaseproof paper and beans and bake for another 5 minutes.

Reduce the oven temperature down to 180°C/350°F/Gas Mark 4.

Mix the sugar, egg yolks and cream together lightly and stir into the apricot purée. Whisk the egg whites until stiff, but not dry, and fold into the purée with a metal spoon. Pour the apricot mixture into the pastry case and bake for 30 minutes.

Serve hot, warm or cool, with or without cream or Vanilla Ice Cream (see page 148).

Apple Cheesecake

Before domestic freezing, fruit was preserved by bottling, making jam or preparing a thick fruit purée called a cheese. This pudding is adapted from an old British recipe and hence is not a cheesecake as we know it today, but a rich apple curd in a crumbly almond pastry.

SERVES 6
use a 23cm/9in loose-based tart tin (see page 180)

For the pastry

175g/6oz plain white flour
25g/1oz ground almonds
100g/4oz butter, chilled and cut into pieces
25g/1oz caster sugar
1 medium egg yolk

For the filling

900g/2lb cooking apples, peeled, cored and cut into pieces
100g/4oz butter
finely grated rind of 1 large lemon
3 tbsp lemon juice
100g/4oz caster sugar
3 medium eggs, lightly beaton

Make the pastry as described on pages 181–2, wrap in greaseproof paper and leave to rest in the fridge for 30 minutes. Line the tart tin (see page 182) and prick the base with a fork. Preheat the oven to 190°C/375°F/Gas Mark 5.

To make the filling, put the apples, butter, lemon rind and juice into a heavy-based saucepan and cook over a low heat, stirring from time to time, until the apples are just tender. Stir in the sugar, then purée. Leave the apple purée to cool a little, then add the eggs. Pour the apple mixture into the pastry case and bake for 40 minutes until the filling has set.

Serve warm or cold with cream, Vanilla Ice Cream (see page 148) or natural yogurt.

BAKEWELL TART WITH FRESH RASPBERRIES

Legend has it that the original Bakewell Tart was made as a mistake by the cook at the Rutland Arms in Bakewell, Derbyshire, who misunderstood her instructions to add butter, eggs and sugar to the jam tart pastry and put them on top instead. Jane Austen is said to have dined at the inn and the tart became extremely popular. However, earlier references to a similar tart have also been traced.

Don't let the often oversweet, commercial versions of Bakewell Tart, made with lots of artificial almond flavouring, put you off trying this version, which is also delicious made without the fresh raspberries.

SERVES 6

use a 23mm/9in loose-based tart tin (see page 180)

For the pastry

175g/6oz plain white flour
75g/3oz butter, chilled and cut into pieces
1 small egg

For the filling

5 tbsp raspberry jam
350g/12oz raspberries
100g/4oz butter, softened
100g/4oz caster sugar
2 large eggs
100g/4oz ground almonds
25g/1oz flaked almonds

Make the pastry and line the tart tin as described on pages 181–2, prick the base with a fork and leave to rest in the fridge for 30 minutes.

Preheat the oven to 200°C/400°F/Gas Mark 6. Spread the jam over the pastry base and scatter over the raspberries.

Put the butter, sugar, eggs and ground almonds into a food processor and process until smooth. Alternatively, cream the butter and sugar together, then lightly beat the eggs and add to the creamed mixture a little at a time. Mix in the ground almonds.

Spread the almond mixture over the raspberries, sprinkle the flaked almonds on top and bake for 35–40 minutes until the filling is risen and golden brown.

Serve warm or cold, with cream or Vanilla Ice Cream (see page 148).

Chocolate Tart

This recipe is based on one from John Farley's *The London Art of Cookery*, first published in 1789, and is a luxurious combination of melting flavours and textures; a crisp hazelnut pastry filled with a rich chocolate cream and covered in a light meringue. The tart must be eaten on the day it is made.

SERVES 6
use a loose-based 23cm/9in tart tin (see page 180)

For the pastry

175g/6oz plain white flour
100g/4oz butter, chilled and cut into pieces
50g/2oz caster sugar
75g/3oz finely chopped, roasted hazelnuts
1 small egg yolk

For the filling

100g/4oz bitter chocolate, grated
475ml/16fl oz cold milk
50g/2oz plain white flour
pinch of salt
50g/2oz caster sugar
10cm/4in cinnamon stick
25g/1oz butter
4 medium egg yolks, lightly beaten
3 tbsp rum

For the meringue

4 medium egg whites
175g/6oz caster sugar

Make the pastry as for the Biscuits on page 175, then wrap in greaseproof paper and leave in the fridge for 30 minutes.

Preheat the oven to 200°C/400°F/Gas Mark 6.

Roll out the pastry on a lightly floured surface, line the tart tin (see page 182), prick the base with a fork and bake the pastry blind (see page 182) for 10 minutes, then remove the greaseproof paper and beans and bake for another 5 minutes.

Reduce the oven temperature to 170°C/325°F/Gas Mark 3.

To make the filling, put the chocolate, milk, flour, salt, sugar and cinnamon stick in a small, heavy-based saucepan. Stir over a very low heat until the chocolate and sugar have melted and the mixture is smooth; then simmer them for 2 minutes. Remove the pan from the heat, add the butter and leave to cool a little. Take out the cinnamon stick and add the egg yolks and the rum. Pour the mixture into the pastry case and bake for 15 minutes.

Reduce the oven temperature to 150°C/300°F/Gas Mark 2.

Whisk the egg whites until stiff, but not dry, whisk in about half the sugar, then fold in the rest with a metal spoon. Pile the meringue over the filling, sealing it to the pastry edge. Bake for a further 30 minutes until the top is golden.

Serve at room temperature, with cream or Vanilla Ice Cream (see page 148).

Currant Curd Cheesecake

A recipe from both John Farley's *The London Art of Cookery*, first published in 1789, and Elizabeth Raffald's *The Experienced English Housekeeper*, first published in 1805. This version uses half the amount of currants.

SERVES 6
use a 23cm/9in loose-based tart tin (see page 180)

For the pastry

175g/6oz plain white flour
75g/3oz butter, chilled and cut into pieces
1 small egg

For the filling

225g/8oz curd cheese
3 tbsp double cream
100g/4oz caster sugar
4 medium eggs, lightly beaten
1 tbsp orange flower water *(see page 179)*
freshly grated nutmeg
100g/4oz currants

Make the pastry and line the tart tin as described on pages 181–2, prick the base with a fork, then leave it to rest in the fridge for 30 minutes.

Preheat the oven to 200°C/400°F/Gas Mark 6.

Bake the pastry blind (see page 182) for 10 minutes, then remove the greaseproof paper and beans and bake for another 5 minutes.

Reduce the oven temperature to 180°C/350°F/Gas Mark 4.

Beat together all the ingredients for the filling except the currants. Arrange the currants evenly in the pastry case, then pour over the curd cheese mixture and bake for 30 minutes.

Serve at room temperature.

Custard Tart

We kept making Custard Tarts following traditional recipes, and found that the results were always exceedingly dull and virtually inedible. Then we added honey and orange flower water, an idea from the eighteenth century much used by Elizabeth Raffald.

SERVES 6
use a 23cm/9in loose-based tart tin (see page 180)

For the pastry

175g/6oz plain white flour
75g/3oz butter, chilled and cut into pieces
1 small egg

For the filling

450ml/¾pint double cream
small blade of mace
3 large eggs
2 tbsp honey
1 tbsp orange flower water (see page 179)

Make the pastry and line the tart tin as described on pages 181–2, prick the base with a fork and leave to rest in the fridge for 30 minutes.

Preheat the oven to 200°C/400°F/Gas Mark 6.

Bake the pastry blind (see page 182) for 10 minutes. Remove the greaseproof paper and beans and bake for another 5 minutes.

Reduce the oven temperature to 170°C/325°F/Gas Mark 3.

Meanwhile, make the filling. Put the cream and mace into a small heavy saucepan, bring slowly to boiling point, then turn off the heat, cover the saucepan with a lid and leave to infuse for 30 minutes.

Lightly beat the eggs, honey and orange flower water together. Take the mace out of the cream, then stir the cream into the egg mixture. Pour into the pastry case and bake for 35 minutes. Serve warm or cold.

Jam Tart with Almond Pastry Lattice

This simple jam tart, made with an excellent crisp almond pastry and a good-quality fruit jam or conserve, makes a really great pudding. Traditionally, criss-cross, spiral or star-shaped pastry patterns were filled with different coloured jams as a means of showing off. A shortcrust pastry using 225g/8oz plain white flour, 100g/4oz butter, chilled and cut into pieces and 1 medium egg can be used instead of the almond pastry. Brush the shortcrust pastry lattice with a little milk before baking.

SERVES 6
use a 23cm/9in pie plate (see page 179)

For the pastry

175g/6oz plain white flour
50g/2oz unblanched almonds, coarsely ground
75g/3oz butter, chilled and cut into pieces
25g/1oz caster sugar
1 small egg

For the filling

finely grated rind of ½ lemon
275g/10oz blackcurrant conserve (or jam of any flavour)

Preheat the oven to 200°C/400°F/Gas Mark 6.

Make the pastry as for the Biscuits on page 175, then wrap the pastry in greaseproof paper and leave in the fridge to rest for 30 minutes.

Roll out just over half of the pastry on a lightly floured surface and line the pie plate. Mix the lemon rind into the jam and spread it over the pastry, leaving a rim of pastry around the edge. Roll out the rest of the pastry and cut it into 2cm/¾in wide strips. Arrange the strips over the jam in a lattice pattern, brushing a little milk on to each end of the strips and pressing them into the pastry rim. Bake for 20–25 minutes.

Serve just warm or cold, with cream, Custard Sauce (see page 173), Vanilla Ice Cream (see page 148) or natural yogurt.

Lemon Cheesecake or Lemon Curd Tart

This is based on a recipe of Mrs Beeton's and has a rich, velvety, fresh-tasting filling. The 'cheese' in the title is an old English word for curd.

SERVES 8
use a 26cm/10¼in loose-based tart tin (see page 180)

For the pastry

225g/8oz plain white flour
100g/4oz butter, chilled and cut into pieces
1 medium egg

For the filling

6 medium eggs, lightly beaten
350g/12oz caster sugar
finely grated rind of 3 large lemons
175ml/6fl oz lemon juice
100g/4oz ground almonds
icing sugar, to serve

Make the pastry and line the tart tin as described on pages 181–2, prick the base with a fork, then leave to rest in the fridge for 30 minutes.

Preheat the oven to 200°C/400°F/Gas Mark 6.

Bake the pastry blind (see page 182) for 10 minutes, then remove the greaseproof paper and beans and bake for another 5 minutes. Reduce the oven temperature to 180°C/350°F/Gas Mark 4.

Make the filling by putting all the ingredients *except* the ground almonds into the top of a double boiler or in a heatproof bowl placed over simmering water. Stir continuously until the curd has thickened, then mix in the almonds and pour the filling into the pastry case.

Bake the tart for 25 minutes until the filling has set, then leave it to cool. Serve at room temperature, dusted with icing sugar at the last minute and with cream.

Parsnip and Ginger Flan

A delicious old-fashioned, meringue-topped flan with a subtle taste of sweet parsnips.

SERVES 6
use a 23cm/9in loose-based tart tin (see page 180)

For the pastry

175g/6oz plain white flour
75g/3oz butter, chilled and cut into pieces
1 small egg

For the filling

675g/1½lb parsnips, peeled and cut into even-sized pieces
2 pieces stem ginger, finely chopped
2 tbsp stem ginger syrup
finely grated rind of 1 lemon
3 tbsp lemon juice
3 large egg yolks, lightly beaten

For the meringue

3 large egg whites
100g/4oz caster sugar

Preheat the oven to 200°C/400°F/Gas Mark 6.

Make the pastry and line the tart tin as described on pages 181–2, prick the base with a fork, then leave in the fridge to rest for 30 minutes.

To make the filling, boil the parsnips in water until they are just tender, then drain and purée them. Stir in the finely chopped stem ginger, ginger syrup, grated lemon rind and juice and the egg yolks. Spoon the mixture into the pastry case and bake for 30 minutes.

Reduce the oven temperature to 150°C/300°F/Gas Mark 2.

For the meringue, whisk the egg whites until they are stiff, but not dry. Whisk in about half the sugar, then fold in the rest with a metal spoon. Pile the meringue over the filling, sealing it to the pastry edge. Bake the flan for a further 30 minutes until the top is golden brown.

Serve warm or cold, with cream or Vanilla Ice Cream (see page 148).

PEAR TART

John Farley writes about Pear Tarts in *The London Art of Cookery* first published in 1789: 'Apples and pears, intended to be put into tarts, must be pared, cut into quarters, and cored. Cut the quarters across again, set them on a saucepan with as much water as will barely cover them, and let them simmer on a slow fire just till the fruit be tender. Put a good piece of lemon-peel into the water with the fruit, and then have your patties ready. Lay fine sugar at the bottom, then your fruit, and a little sugar on top. Pour over each tart a teaspoonful of lemon juice, and three teaspoonfuls of the liquor they were boiled in. Then put on your lid and bake them in a slack oven.'

Our version is made with a rich almond pastry and is flavoured with ratafia biscuits (see page 179). The pastry is very soft and must be rolled out thinly; if it breaks, it can be stuck back together, even after it has been put over the pears.

SERVES 6

use a 23cm/9in pie plate (see page 179)

For the pastry

175g/6oz plain white flour
50g/2oz ground almonds
100g/4oz butter, chilled and cut into pieces
25g/1oz caster sugar
1 small egg yolk

For the fruit

675g/1½lb pears, peeled, cored, quartered and cut across again
strip of lemon rind
25g/1oz ratafia biscuits, quartered (see page 179)
3 tbsp lemon juice
75g/3oz caster sugar

Make the pastry as described on pages 181–2, wrap in greaseproof paper and leave to rest in the fridge for 1 hour.

Put the pears and lemon rind with enough cold water to cover them in a heavy-based saucepan and simmer gently until they are just tender. Remove the lemon rind and strain the fruit, reserving the juice.

Preheat the oven to 200°C/400°F/Gas Mark 6.

Roll out just under half of the pastry on a lightly floured surface and line the pie plate. Sprinkle the ratafia biscuits over the pastry, then heap the pears on top. Pour the lemon juice and a scant 125ml/4fl oz of the reserved pear juice over the fruit, then sprinkle the sugar on top.

Roll out the rest of the pastry to a circle that is a slightly larger than the pie plate. Put the pastry lid over the fruit and press the edge well to seal it, leaving thumb prints around the rim or making shallow indentations with the back of a fork. Trim off any overhanging pastry and bake the pie for 25 minutes until the pastry is golden brown.

Serve warm or cold, with cream, Custard Sauce (see page 173), Vanilla Ice Cream (see page 148) or natural yogurt.

Prune and Apple Tart with Brandy

This recipe has been adapted from the *Manual of Modern Cookery* by Lindsay and Mottram, first published in 1927.

SERVES 6
use a 23cm/9in loose-based tart tin (see page 180)

For the pastry

250g/9oz plain white flour
175g/6oz butter, chilled and cut into pieces
75g/3oz caster sugar
grated rind of ½ lemon • 1 small egg

For the filling

450g/1lb cooking apples, peeled, cored and cut into pieces
175g/6oz stoned prunes, roughly chopped
grated rind of ½ lemon
3 tbsp cold water
100g/4oz soft light brown sugar
3 tbsp brandy • a little cold milk for brushing

Make the pastry as described on pages 181–2, wrap in greaseproof paper and leave to rest in the fridge for 30 minutes. To make the filling, put the apples, prunes, lemon rind and water into a saucepan and cook gently for about 15 minutes until the fruit is just tender. Stir in the sugar and purée the mixture. Leave until completely cold, then stir in the brandy. Preheat the oven to 200°C/400°F/Gas Mark 6.

Roll out two-thirds of the pastry on a lightly floured surface, line the tart tin and prick the base with a fork. Fill the pastry case with the filling. Roll out the rest of the pastry, cut it into 1cm/½in wide strips and make a pastry lattice, brushing a little milk onto each end of the strips and pressing them into the pastry edge. Brush the strips with milk. Bake the tart for 30 minutes. Serve warm or cold, with cream, Custard Sauce (see page 173), Vanilla Ice Cream (see page 148) or natural yogurt.

Treacle Tart

Treacle Tart is one of the cornerstones of British pudding lore. We are always amazed at how these very simple ingredients combine to make such an indulgently delicious pudding. Golden syrup is much easier to handle when it is warm, so if you are using a tin of it, heat the open tin first, in a pan of simmering water, until the syrup becomes runny.

SERVES 6
use a 23cm/9in loose-based tart tin (see page 180)

For the pastry

225g/8oz plain white flour
100g/4oz butter, chilled and cut into pieces
1 medium egg

For the filling

450g/1lb golden syrup
75g/3oz fresh white breadcrumbs
1/4 tsp ground ginger
finely grated rind of 1 lemon
2 tbsp lemon juice
a little cold milk for brushing

Make the pastry and line the tart tin with about two-thirds of the pastry as described on pages 181–2. Prick the base with a fork, then leave to rest in the fridge for 30 minutes, with the remaining pastry wrapped in greaseproof paper. Preheat the oven to 190°C/375°F/Gas Mark 5.

Mix together the golden syrup, breadcrumbs, ginger, lemon rind and juice and leave it to thicken a little. Pour into the pastry case. Roll out the rest of the pastry and cut it into 1cm/1/2in wide strips. Arrange the strips on the tart in a lattice pattern, brushing a little milk onto each end of the strips and pressing them lightly into the pastry rim. Brush the strips with milk and bake the tart for 30 minutes. Serve warm or cold, with cream.

CHAPTER 3

BAKED PUDDINGS

Apple Charlotte
Cluny Pudding
Baked Roly Poly Pudding
Lemon Semolina Pudding
Rice Pudding
Ipswich Almond Pudding
Blackcurrant Pudding
Bread and Butter Pudding
Eve's Pudding
Gooseberry Tansy
Macaroni Pudding with Sultanas and Brandy
Surprise Lemon Puddings
Queen of Puddings

Baked puddings include many of the standard old family favourites, such as Bread and Butter Pudding, Queen of Puddings and Roly Poly Pudding, traditionally given to children and hence full of nostalgia for adults.

However, some people's memories of these puddings are mixed, probably due to the fact that they were not always served at their best in school or nursery. Despite this, many baked puddings have recently been singled out by our top young chefs and lavishly produced in the best restaurants to much acclaim.

Not least, baked puddings tend to be particularly simple to prepare and fill the kitchen with the irresistible scent of baking.

Apple Charlotte

A pudding that is sure to have developed from a windfall of apples and some left-over bread. Several old recipes suggest adding jam or preserved fruit to the apple purée. We have found that using brioche and fruit spread, available in many varieties from wholefood shops, transforms this old-fashioned pudding.

Charlotte moulds can easily be substituted by deep cake tins or soufflé dishes of the same capacity. Make sure that the edges of the brioche pieces are well pressed together or the charlotte will collapse when it is turned out.

SERVES 6

use a 2.4 litre/4 pint charlotte mould or a deep 18cm/7in cake tin

For the filling

1.4kg/3lb cooking apples, peeled, cored and cut into pieces
10cm/4in cinnamon stick
8 whole cloves
50g/2oz unsalted butter
100g/4oz caster sugar, plus a little extra for sprinkling
2 pieces of lemon rind
1 tbsp lemon juice
175g/6oz fruit spread

For lining the mould

1 large brioche loaf, sliced
150g/5oz unsalted butter, melted

Preheat the oven to 200°C/400°F/Gas Mark 6.

Put all the ingredients for the filling, except the fruit spread, into a saucepan and cook over a medium heat, stirring from time to time, until the apples are just tender. Remove the cinnamon stick, cloves and lemon rind and purée the apples.

Meanwhile, melt the unsalted butter, brush the charlotte mould or tin with a little of it, then sprinkle over some sugar. Brush the slices of brioche all over on both sides with the butter and line the charlotte mould, overlapping the pieces slightly to make a good seal. Spoon the fruit spread into the bottom of the lined mould, followed by the apple purée, and cover with a layer of brioche, overlapping the pieces slightly again. Bake the charlotte for 40 minutes, leave in the dish to rest for 5 minutes, then turn out onto a plate and sprinkle over a little more sugar.

Serve warm, with cream, Custard Sauce (see page 173), Vanilla Ice Cream (see page 148) or natural yogurt.

Cluny Pudding

This is based on a recipe from *The Practical Daily Menu* by C.B. Peacock, first published in 1926, and is really a Bread and Butter Pudding delicately flavoured with ginger.

SERVES 4
use a 1.8 litre/3 pint ovenproof dish

butter for greasing
5 slices white buttered bread, crusts removed and quartered
40g/1½oz preserved ginger, finely chopped
2 large eggs
1 tbsp caster sugar
600ml/1 pint cold milk

Preheat the oven to 170°C/325°F/Gas Mark 3 and butter the dish well.

Layer the buttered bread in the dish, sprinkling the preserved ginger evenly between the layers and over the top. Beat the eggs and sugar together and mix in the milk. Pour the mixture over the bread and bake the pudding for 1 hour until golden brown.

Serve warm, with cream.

BAKED ROLY POLY PUDDING

A warming winter pudding, well known to Thackeray and Dickens as great comforting British food. It can also be made with golden syrup and a little ground ginger instead of the jam and lemon rind.

SERVES 4–6
use a baking sheet

175g/6oz white self-raising flour
75g/3oz shredded suet (see page 179)
about 120ml/4fl oz cold water
finely grated rind of 1 lemon
225g/8oz fruit jam

Preheat the oven to 180°C/350°F/Gas Mark 4.

Mix the flour and suet together in a large mixing bowl, then stir in the water to make a soft dough. Roll out the dough on a lightly floured surface to an oblong that is twice as long as it is wide and about 5mm/¼in thick.

Mix the lemon rind into the jam and spread it evenly over the suet crust, leaving a 25mm/1in border around the edge. Roll up the long edge of the suet crust like a Swiss Roll, then pinch the open ends together.

Wrap the pudding loosely in a piece of buttered foil, place on the baking sheet and bake it for 50 minutes.

Serve immediately with Custard Sauce (see page 173).

LEMON SEMOLINA PUDDING

Discussing *Great British Puddings* at a dinner party of old friends recently, there was a groan all round when semolina was mentioned. This is, however, a marvellously light and lemony pudding recipe from Eliza Acton's *Modern Cookery for Private Families*, first published in 1845, which triumphs over its dire reputation, and is definitely *nothing* like the lumpy semolina many of us associate with school dinners.

SERVES 6–8
use a 2.4 litre/4 pint ovenproof dish

65g/2½oz semolina
900ml/1½ pints cold milk
50g/2oz butter, plus a little extra for greasing
75g/3oz caster sugar • finely grated rind of 1 lemon
5 medium eggs

Preheat the oven to 180°C/350°F/Gas Mark 4 and butter the dish well.

Put the semolina and milk into a heavy-based saucepan, bring to the boil and simmer for 8–10 minutes, stirring continuously. Take the pan off the heat and mix in the butter, sugar and lemon rind. Leave the mixture to cool a little, then beat in the eggs. Pour the semolina into the dish and bake for 45 minutes until the pudding is set and golden brown.

Serve with poached fruit or fruit conserve.

Rice Pudding

One of the simplest and most delicious British puddings, immortalised by A. A. Milne in *When We Were Very Young* (1924):

'What is the matter with Mary Jane?
She's perfectly well and she hasn't a pain,
And it's lovely rice pudding for dinner again!
What is the matter with Mary Jane?'

Creamier milk makes a creamier pudding, but we tend to use semi-skimmed milk which is perfectly OK.

SERVES 4–6
use a 1.5 litre/2½ pint ovenproof dish

75g/3oz short-grain pudding rice
50g/2oz sugar
25g/1oz butter, cut into small pieces, plus a little extra for greasing
1.2 litres/2 pints cold milk
freshly grated nutmeg

Preheat the oven to 150°C/300°F/Gas Mark 2. Lightly butter the dish.

Put the rice, sugar and butter into the dish and pour over the milk. Stir the mixture briefly, then grate some nutmeg over the top. Bake the pudding for 3 hours, stirring in the skin 3 times, once every 30 minutes for the first hour and a half, then leave the pudding to cook until it is creamy and golden brown on top.

Serve warm or cold, with cream.

Ipswich Almond Pudding

Ipswich Almond Pudding is described in both John Farley's *The London Art of Cookery* (1789) and *The Compleat Housewife* by Eliza Smith (1758). The recipes are very similar, although John Farley's is baked in a puff pastry crust. This version is really like a delicate almond soufflé with a creamy centre.

SERVES 6

use a 2.4 litre/4 pint ovenproof dish

generous 40g/1½oz fresh white breadcrumbs
450ml/¾ pint single cream
100g/4oz ground almonds
2 tbsp orange flower water (see page 179)
4 medium egg yolks, lightly beaten
50g/2oz caster sugar
50g/2oz butter, melted, plus a little extra for greasing
2 medium egg whites

Soak the breadcrumbs in the cream for 30 minutes. Butter the dish well.

Preheat the oven to 180°C/350°F/Gas Mark 4.

Mix together the almonds, orange flower water, egg yolks, sugar and melted butter, then stir in the breadcrumbs and cream. Whisk the egg whites until stiff, but not dry, and fold into the mixture with a metal spoon. Pour the mixture into the dish and bake for 30 minutes.

Serve warm, with cream.

Blackcurrant Pudding

Our friend Janice was given a handwritten book of recipes by her mother, Greta Dilley, when she left home. One of the recipes is called Devonshire Apple Cake which she makes with 450g/1lb apples, peeled, cored and finely chopped. She also suggests using blackcurrants, as in the following recipe, which makes a wonderfully fragrant, warm pudding for cool summer days.

SERVES 4–5
use a 1.8 litre/3 pint ovenproof dish

50g/2oz butter, softened, plus a little extra for greasing
75g/3oz caster sugar, plus a little extra for sprinkling
2 small eggs, beaten
100g/4oz self-raising flour, sifted
pinch of salt
225g/8oz blackcurrants, stripped from the stalk

Preheat the oven to 180°C/350°F/Gas Mark 4 and butter the dish well.

Beat the butter and sugar together until they are light and fluffy. Whisk in the eggs, then add the flour and salt. Fold in the blackcurrants and transfer the mixture to the dish.

Bake the pudding for 45 minutes until golden brown, testing that the centre is cooked with a skewer. Leave the pudding in the dish to rest for 5 minutes, then turn it out onto a warm plate and sprinkle with a little more sugar.

Serve warm, with cream, Vanilla Ice Cream (see page 148) or natural yogurt.

Bread and Butter Pudding

Bread and Butter Pudding has, for a long time, been thought of as a quaint British nursery pudding, but it has recently made a triumphant come back and is now a favourite with many of the fashionable British chefs. It is sometimes served with the additions of marmalade, lemon curd, apples, oranges, spice, honey or caramel. This is a classic version which is hard to beat.

SERVES 5–6
use a 1.8 litre/3 pint ovenproof dish

butter for greasing
8 medium slices buttered white bread, crusts removed and quartered
100g/4oz currants or sultanas
3 large eggs
50g/2oz sugar
finely grated rind of 1 lemon
600ml/1 pint cold milk
1 vanilla pod
1 tbsp demerara sugar

Butter the dish well and arrange the bread, butter side up, in the dish, layering it with the currants or sultanas.

Lightly beat the eggs with the sugar and lemon rind. Place the milk in a saucepan with the vanilla pod, bring to boiling point, cover with a lid and leave to infuse for 30 minutes. Remove the vanilla pod and pour the milk over the eggs and sugar stirring well. Pour the milk mixture over the bread and butter and leave the pudding to stand for about 1 hour.

Preheat the oven to 180°C/350°F/Gas Mark 4.

Sprinkle the demerara sugar on top of the pudding and bake for 45–50 minutes until risen and golden brown.

Serve warm, with cream.

Eve's Pudding

A comforting, spiced apple family pudding with a light sponge topping.

SERVES 6
use a 2.4 litre/4 pint ovenproof dish

For the apples

675g/1½lb cooking apples, peeled, cored and thinly sliced
3 generous tbsp honey
finely grated rind of ½ lemon
1 tsp ground cinnamon
2 tbsp cold water

For the sponge

100g/4oz butter, softened, plus a little extra for greasing
100g/4oz caster sugar
175g/6oz white self-raising flour
2 large eggs
1 tbsp cold milk

Preheat the oven to 180°C/350°F/Gas Mark 4. Butter the dish well.

Put the apples into the dish, mix in the honey, lemon rind, cinnamon and water, then level the fruit.

To make the sponge, put the butter, sugar, flour, eggs and milk into a food processor and process the mixture until it is smooth. Alternatively, beat the mixture until it is smooth in an electric mixer, or by hand with a wooden spoon. Pour the batter evenly over the apples, spreading it to the edge of the dish, and bake the pudding for 50 minutes until risen and golden brown.

Serve warm or cold, with cream, Custard Sauce (see page 173), Vanilla Ice Cream (see page 148) or natural yogurt.

Gooseberry Tansy

This dish dates back to the fifteenth century and was originally a type of omelette, using the rather bitter herb tansy for its medicinal qualities. It has evolved over the centuries into a light mousse-like pudding, made with fruit purée, cream and eggs. Our version is quite wintry and can be made with frozen gooseberries.

SERVES 6
use a 2.4 litre/4 pint ovenproof dish

675g/1½lb gooseberries, topped and tailed
50g/2oz butter, plus a little extra for greasing
piece of lemon rind
100g/4oz caster sugar, plus a little extra for sprinkling
100g/4oz fresh white breadcrumbs
150ml/¼ pint double cream
4 large eggs, separated

Preheat the oven to 200°C/400°F/Gas Mark 6 and lightly butter the dish.

Put the gooseberries, butter, lemon rind and sugar into a saucepan and cook for about 10 minutes until the fruit is just soft. Remove the lemon rind, purée the gooseberry mixture and allow to cool a little. Mix in the breadcrumbs, cream and egg yolks. Beat the egg whites until they are stiff, but not dry, then fold them into the mixture with a metal spoon.

Pour the mixture into the dish, sprinkle with a little more sugar and bake for 35 minutes until risen and golden brown.

Serve warm, with cream, Custard Sauce (see page 173), Vanilla Ice Cream (see page 148) or natural yogurt.

Macaroni Pudding with Sultanas and Brandy

Our families were rather reluctant to try this pudding. Like many people, they'd had dreadful experiences of macaroni pudding at school, and could not believe that it would be anything other than an ordeal. They were, however, knocked out by the delicate sophistication of this dish. It is a mellow milk pudding based on a recipe both in Mrs Beeton's *Book of Household Management* (1861) and in D. Williamson's *The Practice of Cookery and Pastry* (1896).

SERVES 6
use a 2.1 litre/3½ pint ovenproof dish

100g/4oz sultanas
2 tbsp brandy
100g/4oz macaroni
1.2 litres/2 pints cold milk
strip of lemon rind
50g/2oz butter, cut into pieces, plus a little extra for greasing
50g/2oz soft light brown sugar
3 large eggs, lightly beaten

Put the sultanas and brandy in a bowl and leave to soak for about 1 hour. Lightly butter the dish.

Preheat the oven to 180°C/350°F/Gas Mark 4.

Boil the macaroni in the milk, with the strip of lemon rind, for 20 minutes or until the macaroni is tender, stirring from time to time. Leave the macaroni to cool a little, remove the rind, then stir in the butter, sugar, eggs and sultanas in brandy. Mix together well and pour the mixture into the ovenproof dish. Bake the pudding for 30 minutes until the top is golden brown.

Serve warm or cold, with cream.

Surprise Lemon Puddings

The surprise of this pudding is that it rises like a soufflé, making its own lemon sauce at the bottom of the dish.

SERVES 6
use 6 large ramekins 80mm/3¼in in diameter and 45mm/1¾in high

50g/2oz butter, softened, plus a little extra for greasing
75g/3oz caster sugar
finely grated rind of 1 large lemon
3 tbsp lemon juice
2 large egg yolks
25g/1oz plain white flour
300ml/½ pint cold milk
2 large egg whites

Preheat the oven to 180°C/350°F/Gas Mark 4 and generously butter 6 ramekins.

Beat the butter and sugar together with the lemon rind until light and fluffy, then beat in the lemon juice and egg yolks, followed by the flour and milk.

Whisk the egg whites until stiff, but not dry, then fold into the mixture with a metal spoon and pour into the ramekins. Place the ramekins in a roasting tin with enough boiling water to reach about halfway up their sides and cook for 20–25 minutes until the puddings are well risen and golden brown.

Serve immediately, with cream.

Queen of Puddings

A gentle nursery pudding, guaranteed to bring back memories of childhood. In Wales this is called Monmouth Pudding.

SERVES 6
use a 1.8 litre/3 pint ovenproof dish

For the pudding

100g/4oz fresh white breadcrumbs
25g/1oz caster sugar
finely grated rind of 1 large or 2 small lemons
600ml/1 pint cold milk
50g/2oz butter, cut into pieces, plus a little extra for greasing
4 medium egg yolks, lightly beaten
4 generous tbsp raspberry jam

For the meringue

4 medium egg whites
100g/4oz caster sugar

Preheat the oven to 180°C/350°F/Gas Mark 4. Butter the dish well.

Mix the breadcrumbs, sugar and lemon rind for the pudding together in a large bowl. Heat the milk with the butter to just below boiling point, then pour over the breadcrumb mixture. Leave the mixture to cool a little, stir in the egg yolks, then pour into the ovenproof dish. Bake the pudding for 30 minutes until it is just set. Warm the jam and spread it carefully over the pudding.

To make the meringue, whisk the egg whites until they are stiff, but not dry, then whisk in about half the sugar. Fold in the rest of the sugar, with a metal spoon. Pile the meringue on top of the pudding and return to the oven for 15 minutes until the meringue is golden brown.

Serve warm, with cream.

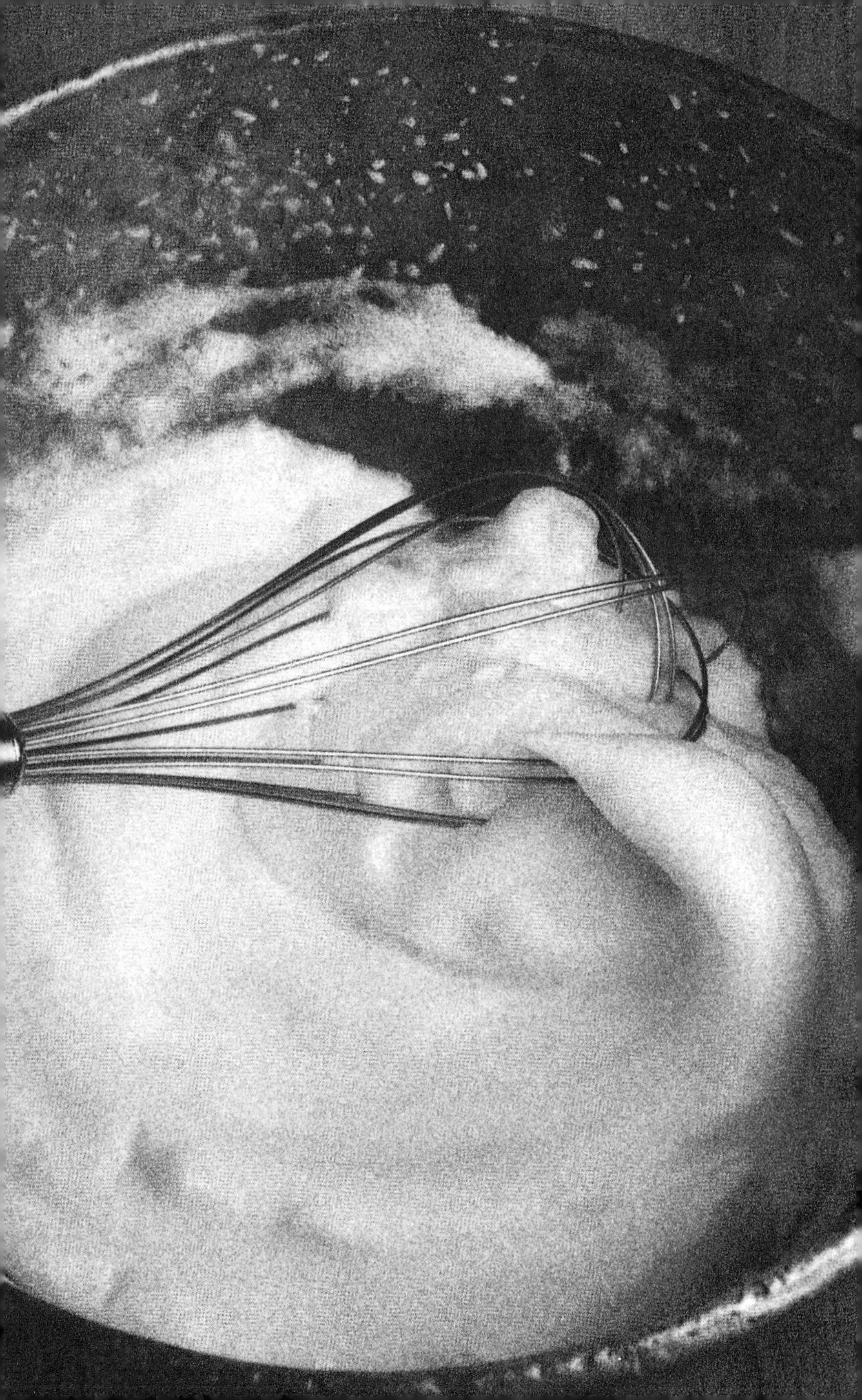

CHAPTER 4

STEAMED PUDDINGS

Blackberry Pudding
Black Cap Pudding
Cabinet Pudding
Carrot and Orange Pudding
Eliza Acton's Christmas Pudding
Export Christmas Pudding
Ginger Pudding
A Bachelor's Pudding
Spotted Dick
Rice and Gooseberry Pudding
Mrs Beeton's Golden Marmalade Pudding
Light Chocolate Pudding
Sussex Pond Pudding
Orange (or Lemon) Sponge Pudding
Sticky Toffee Pudding
Treacle or Jam Sponge Pudding
Walnut and Apple Pudding

We are impassioned devotees of the steamed pudding. It is a dish of infinite paradox: dauntingly heavy by reputation yet wonderfully light and airy if made properly. Steaming a pudding may seem to be a lengthy process, but the great advantage is that it can be prepared well in advance and forgotten about while it is bubbling away. Steamed puddings, whether sponge, suet crust or batter puddings, are the ultimate comfort food on damp winter days.

Clearly, from the many references in old cookery books, the steamed pudding has had a long and varied reign. The affectionate names bestowed on it over the years tell the story eloquently. Eliza Acton gave us Publisher's Pudding, Author's Pudding and the Elegant Economist's Pudding. Mrs Beeton responded with Aunt Martha's Pudding, Aunt Polly's Pudding and the resoundingly contemporary Queer Times Pudding.

The king of British steamed puddings is of course the Christmas Pudding. Charles Dickens immortalised it in A Christmas Carol*: 'Mrs Cratchit entered – flushed, but smiling proudly – with the pudding, like a speckled cannon-ball, so hard and firm, blazing in half-a-quartern of ignited brandy, and bedight with Christmas holly stuck into the top. Oh, a wonderful pudding!'*

Blackberry Pudding

This is a traditional, steamed suet crust family pudding. It can be filled with any type of fruit; however, we found blackberries were particularly successful. Although it is now easy to buy cultivated blackberries, this pudding is definitely best made with wild ones, which tend to have more flavour.

SERVES 6
use a 1.2 litre/2 pint pudding basin

butter for greasing
225g/8oz white self-raising flour
100g/4oz shredded suet (see page 179)
about 150ml/¼ pint cold water
450g/1lb blackberries
100g/4oz caster sugar

Butter the pudding basin well. Mix together the flour and suet in a large bowl, then add the water and mix to a soft dough.

Roll out two-thirds of the dough on a lightly floured surface and use to line the basin. Mix the blackberries with the sugar and put into the pudding basin. Roll out the remaining third of dough, brush the edge with a little water and place on top of the fruit, pressing well around the rim of the dough to seal. Cover and steam (see pages 180–81) for 3 hours. Leave the pudding to stand for 2–3 minutes before turning out onto a warm dish.

Serve immediately, with cream, Custard Sauce (see page 173), Vanilla Ice Cream (see page 148) or natural yogurt.

Black Cap Pudding

We were surprised to find quite so many variations of this recipe in old cookery books, especially as most of them did not seem to work. However, this version, from *Warne's Everyday Cookery* by Mrs Mabel Wijey, rewritten in the 1950s, is light and creamy and makes an unusual, very simple family pudding. It must not be left standing around, but cooked immediately, steamed over very low heat and eaten without delay. As the only sweetness in the pudding is from the currants, it is important to serve each person with both the batter and some currants, and to eat a little of each at the same time.

SERVES 4–5
use a 1.2 litre/2 pint pudding basin

butter for greasing
75g/3oz white self-raising flour
pinch of salt
3 large eggs
600ml/1 pint cold milk
25g/1oz butter, melted
100g/4oz currants

Butter the pudding basin well. Put the flour and salt into a large bowl and mix in the eggs. Gradually add the milk to make a smooth batter, then beat the batter thoroughly for several minutes. Stir in the melted butter and the currants. Pour the mixture into the pudding basin, cover and steam (see pages 180–81) for 1½ hours. Turn out onto a warm dish.

Serve immediately.

Cabinet Pudding

Old illustrations of this recipe show the raisins and rind arranged in neat rows up the side of the pudding, which is a bit fiddly to do, but looks very good when the pudding is turned out. Most of the original recipes use candied citron rind. However, candied orange rind has more flavour *and* is less anaemic looking. Often, glacé cherries were used as well, but they do not seem to have quite the same appeal nowadays. A deliciously luxurious, old-fashioned steamed pudding anyway, however it is decorated.

SERVES 6–7
use a 1.2 litre/2 pint pudding basin

softened butter for greasing
75g/3oz raisins
75g/3oz candied orange rind, cut into thin strips
225g/8oz sponge cake, sliced
50g/2oz ratafia biscuits (see page 179)
4 medium eggs
25g/1oz caster sugar
600ml/1 pint cold milk
finely grated rind of 1 lemon
5 tbsp brandy

Butter the pudding basin well with a thick layer of softened butter. Press the raisins and candied orange rind into the butter to line the inside of the pudding basin, then fill it with layers of sponge cake and ratafia biscuits.

Lightly beat the eggs and sugar together. Heat the milk to boiling point and pour it over the sugar and eggs, stirring well. Add the lemon rind and the brandy and pour the mixture slowly into the pudding basin. Cover and steam the pudding (see pages 180–81) for 1½ hours. Leave the pudding to stand for 2–3 minutes before turning out onto a warm dish.

Serve hot or cold, with Custard Sauce (see page 173) or cream.

Carrot and Orange Pudding

A lovely, light, steamed pudding which should appeal even to people who don't like carrots.

SERVES 4–6
use a 1.2 litre/2 pint pudding basin

butter for greasing
225g/8oz fresh white breadcrumbs
100g/4oz shredded suet (see page 179)
350g/12oz carrots, peeled or scraped and finely grated
100g/4oz raisins
100g/4oz currants
75g/3oz light muscovado sugar
½ tsp ground cinnamon
3 large eggs, lightly beaten
finely grated rind of 1 large orange
3 tbsp orange juice
3 tbsp sherry
2 tbsp cold milk

Butter the pudding basin well. Mix together the dry ingredients, then stir in the eggs, orange rind and juice, sherry and milk. Put the mixture into the pudding basin, cover and steam (see pages 180–81) for 2½ hours.

Leave the pudding to stand for about 5 minutes before turning out onto a warm dish.

Serve hot, with cream, Custard Sauce (see page 173), Vanilla Ice Cream (see page 148) or natural yogurt.

ELIZA ACTON'S CHRISTMAS PUDDING

This light Christmas pudding is a good alternative for anyone who does not like the rich version.

The following quantity will make a *total* of 1.5 litres/2½ pints, but can be divided between any combination of pudding basin sizes. For the servings per basin size, see Export Christmas Pudding on page 76.

To ignite a Christmas pudding, heat some brandy in a small saucepan, pour it over the hot, turned-out pudding and set it alight.

SERVES 6–8
use a 1.5 litre/2½ pint pudding basin

butter for greasing
75g/3oz plain white flour, sifted
75g/3oz fresh white breadcrumbs
175g/6oz shredded suet (see page 179)
175g/6oz raisins
175g/6oz currants
150g/5oz dark muscovado sugar
50g/2oz candied orange peel, chopped finely
100g/4oz grated cooking apple
½ tsp ground mixed spice
pinch of salt
120ml/4fl oz brandy, plus extra to serve (see above)
3 medium eggs, lightly beaten

Lightly butter the pudding basin. Mix together all the dry ingredients, stirring in each one as it is added, then mix in the brandy, followed by the eggs. Stir together well, then pour the mixture into the pudding basin. Cover and steam (see pages 180–81) for 3½ hours.

Leave the pudding until it is completely cold, then re-cover it with greaseproof paper and foil. Store the pudding in a cool dark place until required, then steam for a further 2–2½ hours. Leave the pudding to stand for 2–3 minutes before turning out onto a warm dish.

Serve hot, with Port Wine Sauce (see page 174), Brandy Sauce (see page 172), or Brandy or Rum Butter (see page 171).

EXPORT CHRISTMAS PUDDING

This is a recipe for a rich, dark, fruity Christmas pudding that has been handed down from father to son, or rather from grandfather to father, of our great friend Bernie Rands. Her grandfather made the Christmas puddings for Meredith and Drew in the 1930s, when many of them were sent to families in the Colonies. The original recipe is for 60 puddings, but we have reduced the quantities to make a total of about 6 litres/10 pints. This can be used to fill any combination of pudding basin sizes. As a *rough* guideline, a 1.8 litre/3 pint pudding will serve 8–9, a 1.2 litre/2 pint pudding will serve 6–7, and a 600ml/1 pint pudding will serve 3–4.

A very large mixing bowl is essential because there are a lot of ingredients and they need to be stirred very well. This is a good reason to encourage friends and family to perpetuate the tradition of each giving 12 good stirs of the pudding before making a wish. The puddings can be kept for up to a year, but are probably best after a couple of months.

Christmas puddings are usually served ignited. To do this heat some brandy in a small saucepan, pour it over the hot, turned-out pudding and set it alight.

MAKES A TOTAL OF 6 litres/10 pints (see above)

450g/1lb currants
450g/1lb sultanas
1kg/2¼lb raisins
175g/6oz candied lemon rind, chopped
150g/5oz candied orange rind, chopped
150g/5oz candied citron rind, chopped
100g/4oz blanched almonds, chopped
100g/4oz white self-raising flour
450g/1lb fresh white breadcrumbs
450g/1lb shredded suet (see page 179)
225g/8oz dark muscovado sugar
225g/8oz caster sugar
2 tbsp ground mixed spice
freshly grated nutmeg

¼ tsp salt
3 large eggs, lightly beaten
175ml/6fl oz cold milk
175ml/6fl oz lemon juice
350ml/12fl oz Guinness
3 tbsp brandy or rum, plus extra brandy to serve (see above)
butter for greasing

Mix the dry ingredients together in a large bowl, then stir in the eggs, milk, lemon juice, Guinness and brandy or rum. Make sure that all the ingredients are really well mixed, then leave the mixture to stand for about 30 minutes.

Grease the pudding basins (see above), spoon the mixture into them, then cover and steam (see pages 180–81) for 4 hours. Leave the puddings until they are completely cold, then re-cover them with greaseproof paper and foil. Store in a cool dark place until required, then steam for a further 2–2½ hours. Leave the puddings to stand for 2–3 minutes before turning out onto a warm dish.

Serve hot, with Brandy Sauce, (see page 172), or Brandy or Rum Butter (see page 171).

GINGER PUDDING

A warming steamed pudding, covered with preserved ginger and preserved ginger syrup.

SERVES 6–8
use a 1.2 litre/2 pint pudding basin

175g/6oz butter, softened, plus extra for greasing
50g/2oz preserved ginger, cut into thin strips
2 tbsp preserved ginger syrup
2 tbsp golden syrup
175g/6oz light muscovado sugar
finely grated rind of 1 lemon
3 tbsp cold milk
3 large eggs
175g/6oz white self-raising flour, sifted
1 heaped tsp ground ginger

Butter the pudding basin thickly with softened butter, then press the strips of preserved ginger evenly into the butter all over the inside of the basin. Pour the preserved ginger syrup and the golden syrup into the bottom of the basin.

Cream the butter and sugar together until light and fluffy, then add the lemon rind and milk. Beat in one egg at a time, whisking the mixture very well after each addition; do not worry if it curdles. Add about half the flour and the ground ginger, then fold in the rest of the flour with a metal spoon. Put the mixture into the basin, level the surface, then cover and steam the pudding (see pages 180–81) for 2½ hours. Leave the pudding to stand for 2–3 minutes before turning out onto a warm dish.

Serve immediately with cream, Custard Sauce (see page 173) or Vanilla Ice Cream (see page 148).

VARIATION

Instead of one large pudding, this can be made in 6 individual 175g/6oz pudding basins. Butter the basins well and divide 50g/2oz preserved ginger, cut into thin strips, 2 tbsp preserved ginger syrup and 2 tbsp golden syrup between them. For the pudding mixture use 100g/4oz butter, softened, 100g/4oz light muscovado sugar, finely grated rind of about 2/3 lemon, 2 tbsp cold milk, 2 large eggs, 100g/4oz white self-raising flour, sifted and 1 tsp ground ginger. Cover the puddings individually (see pages 180–81) and bake in a roasting tin with enough boiling water to reach about halfway up their sides, for 40 minutes, at 190°C/375°F/Gas Mark 5.

A Bachelor's Pudding

A lovely light steamed pudding from Mrs Beeton, made without any fat.

SERVES 4
use a 900ml/1½ pint pudding basin

butter for greasing
100g/4oz fresh white breadcrumbs
100g/4oz currants
100g/4oz grated apple
50g/2oz caster sugar
3 medium eggs, beaten
finely grated rind of ½ lemon
freshly grated nutmeg

Butter the pudding basin well. Mix all the pudding ingredients together and put into the basin. Cover and steam the pudding (see pages 180–81) for 3 hours. Leave the pudding to stand for 2–3 minutes before turning out onto a warm dish.

Serve immediately with Custard Sauce (see page 173) or cream.

Spotted Dick

Probably one of the most famous of all traditional suet puddings, sometimes called Spotted Dog.

SERVES 6–8

350g/12oz self-raising flour
150g/5oz shredded suet (see page 179)
100g/4oz sugar, plus a little extra for sprinkling
175g/6oz currants
350ml/12fl oz cold water

Sift the flour into a large bowl, then stir in the suet, sugar and currants. Pour in the water and mix to a soft dough. Shape the dough into a long sausage and wrap in greaseproof paper.

Scald a clean tea towel and sprinkle it with flour. Roll the pudding loosely in the cloth and tie up each end. Immerse the pudding in boiling water and simmer for 2 hours, leaving enough room in the pan for the pudding to expand.

Serve, sprinkled with a little sugar and Custard Sauce (see page 173).

Rice and Gooseberry Pudding

Don't be put off by the strange method or appearance of this delectable dish from Eliza Acton's *Modern Cookery for Private Families*, first published in 1845.

SERVES 4

175g/6oz short-grain pudding rice
450g/1lb green gooseberries, topped and tailed
about 50g/2oz caster sugar
about 1 tbsp preserved ginger syrup

Scald a clean tea towel and flour it well. Spread the rice over the cloth, then cover the rice with the gooseberries. Tie up the cloth, leaving room for the rice to expand and immerse in a large pan of boiling water. Boil for 1¼ hours. Turn out the pudding onto a warm dish (preferably not a white one).

Serve immediately, strewn with sugar, drizzled with a little ginger syrup and some cream, or serve cold if you're a cold rice pudding fan (also with the sugar, ginger syrup and cream).

Mrs Beeton's Golden Marmalade Pudding

An old-fashioned, suet steamed pudding.

SERVES 6
use a 1.2 litre/2 pint pudding basin

butter for greasing
100g/4oz fresh white breadcrumbs
100g/4oz shredded suet (see page 179)
100g/4oz light muscovado sugar
100g/4oz marmalade
4 medium eggs, lightly beaten

Butter the pudding basin well. Mix together all the rest of the ingredients, adding the beaten eggs last. Put the mixture into the pudding basin, cover and steam (see pages 180–81) for 2 hours. Leave the pudding to stand for 2–3 minutes before turning out onto a warm dish.

Serve immediately, sprinkled with a little caster sugar and Custard Sauce (see page 173).

Light Chocolate Pudding

This recipe seems to have been specially marked by the original owner in our copy of D. Williamson's *The Practice of Cookery and Pastry* and is a deliciously light, steamed chocolate pudding, with a soufflé-like texture.

SERVES 6
use a 1.2 litre/2 pint pudding basin

butter for greasing
75g/3oz bitter chocolate, grated
25g/1oz plain white flour
600ml/1 pint cold milk
50g/2oz fresh white breadcrumbs
4 large eggs, separated
50g/2oz caster sugar, plus a little extra for sprinkling

Butter the pudding basin well. Mix together the grated chocolate and the flour in a saucepan, pour over the milk and bring slowly to the boil, stirring all the time. Boil the mixture for 1 minute, then pour it over the breadcrumbs and leave to cool.

Beat the egg yolks and sugar together by hand, or with an electric mixer, until they are pale and thick, then stir them into the chocolate mixture.

Whisk the egg whites until they are stiff, but not dry, and fold them into the pudding with a metal spoon. Pour the mixture into the pudding basin, cover and steam (see pages 180–81) for 1½ hours. Leave the pudding to stand for 2–3 minutes before turning out onto a warm dish.

Serve immediately, with cream and a little caster sugar sprinkled on top.

Sussex Pond Pudding

A glorious steamed pudding with a rich golden sauce that makes a pond around the pudding when it is cut open. Turn the pudding out onto a deep plate to serve it and give each person a piece of lemon.

If the raw filling does not quite reach to the top of the pudding basin, place the lid directly on top of the filling and seal the lid onto the side of the suet crust, rather than at the top of the basin with air beneath it, or the whole thing will collapse. It is important to use a thin-skinned lemon and pierce it deeply with a skewer.

SERVES 4–6
use a 1.2 litre/2 pint pudding basin

225g/8oz white self-raising flour
100g/4oz shredded suet (see page 179)
scant 150ml/¼ pint cold water, plus a little extra for sealing
100g/4oz butter, diced, plus extra for greasing
100g/4oz light soft brown sugar
1 medium thin-skinned lemon, rinsed and pierced all over with a skewer

Butter the pudding basin well. Mix the flour, suet and water together to make a soft dough. Roll out two-thirds of the dough on a floured surface to about 5mm/¼in thick and line the pudding basin. Roll out the remaining third of dough for the pudding lid.

Put half of the butter and sugar into the lined pudding basin with the lemon in the centre, followed by the rest of the butter and sugar. Brush the rim of the dough lid with a little cold water, cover the pudding and press the edges together well to seal (see above).

Cover and steam the pudding (see pages 180–81) for 3½ hours. Leave the pudding to stand for 2–3 minutes before turning out onto a warm dish.

Serve immediately, with cream.

Orange (or Lemon) Sponge Pudding

This is a light steamed sponge pudding with an orange curd sauce.

SERVES 6–8
use a 1.2 litre/2 pint pudding basin

For the curd

3 medium eggs, lightly beaten
100g/4oz caster sugar • 100g/4oz butter, cut into pieces
finely grated rind of 2 large oranges
175ml/6fl oz orange juice

For the pudding

175g/6oz butter, softened, plus a little extra for greasing
175g/6oz caster sugar
finely grated rind of 1 large orange
3 tbsp cold milk • 3 large eggs
175g/6oz self-raising flour, sifted

To make the curd, put the eggs, sugar, butter, orange rind and juice in the top of a double boiler, or in a bowl over simmering water. Stir continuously until the mixture has thickened.

Butter the pudding basin well. To make the pudding, cream the butter and sugar together until light and fluffy, then add the orange rind and milk. Beat in one egg at a time, whisking very well after each addition; do not worry if it curdles. Add about half the flour, then fold in the rest with a metal spoon. Put the mixture into the basin, level the surface, then cover and steam the pudding (see pages 180–81) for 2½ hours. Leave the pudding to stand for 2–3 minutes before turning out onto a warm dish.

Pour the curd over the pudding and serve immediately, with cream.

VARIATION

For a Lemon Sponge Pudding, make the Lemon Curd on page 45, and substitute lemon rind for the orange rind in the pudding.

Sticky Toffee Pudding

Colin Webb, our lovely publisher, suggested that this recipe was included in our book at the very first meeting. Our hearts sank. We had never tasted it and it sounded *so* sweet and sickly, but we thought that we ought at least to try it. We retract completely. This is a heavenly, *light* pudding. Don't be put off by its dark appearance or name.

SERVES 6–8
use a 1.2 litre/2 pint pudding basin

For the sauce

100g/4oz butter
225g/8oz dark muscovado sugar
150ml/¼ pint double cream
1 tbsp lemon juice

For the pudding

175g/6oz stoned dates, roughly chopped
75g/3oz butter, softened, plus a little extra for greasing
100g/4oz caster sugar
finely grated rind of 1 lemon
2 large eggs
175g/6oz white self-raising flour, sifted
½ tsp bicarbonate of soda

To make the sauce, put the butter, sugar, cream and lemon juice into a saucepan and stir over a low heat until the butter has melted and the sugar dissolved.

Meanwhile, put the dates into a bowl, cover them with boiling water and leave to cool. Butter the pudding basin well. Beat the butter and sugar together until light and fluffy, then beat in the lemon rind. Beat in one egg at a time, whisking the mixture very well after each addition; do not worry if it curdles.

Mix in about half the flour, the bicarbonate of soda and the dates with their soaking water, then fold in the rest of the flour with a metal spoon.

Pour about half the sauce into the bottom of the pudding basin followed by the pudding mixture. Level the surface, then cover and steam the pudding (see pages 180–81) for 2½ hours. Leave the pudding to stand for 2–3 minutes before turning out onto a warm dish. Warm the rest of the sauce and pour it over the top.

Serve immediately, with or without cream.

VARIATION

Instead of one large pudding, this can be made in 8 individual 175ml/6oz pudding basins. Butter them well and put about 1 tbsp sauce into each basin, followed by the pudding mixture. Cover the puddings individually (see pages 180–81) and bake in a roasting tin with enough boiling water to reach about halfway up their sides, for 40 minutes, at 190°C/375°F/Gas Mark 5.

Treacle or Jam Sponge Pudding

SERVES 6–8
use a 1.2 litre/2 pint pudding basin

For the sauce

6 tbsp golden syrup or *raspberry jam*
2 tbsp lemon juice

For the pudding

175g/6oz butter, softened, plus a little extra for greasing
175g/6oz caster sugar
finely grated rind of ½ lemon
3 tbsp cold milk
3 large eggs
175g/6oz white self-raising flour, sifted

Butter the pudding basin well. Mix the golden syrup *or* jam with the lemon juice and pour it into the bottom of the pudding basin.

Cream the butter and sugar together until light and fluffy, then add the lemon rind and milk. Beat in one egg at a time, whisking the mixture very well after each addition; do not worry if it curdles. Add about half the flour, then fold in the rest with a metal spoon. Pour the mixture into the basin, level the surface, then cover and steam the pudding (see pages 180–81) for 2½ hours. Leave the pudding to stand for 2–3 minutes, before turning out onto a warm dish. Serve immediately, with Custard Sauce (see page 173).

VARIATION

To make 6 individual steamed puddings in 175g/6oz pudding basins, use the same amount of golden syrup or jam for the sauce, but only 100g/4oz butter, sugar and flour with 2 large eggs, 2 tbsp milk and the finely grated rind of about ⅓ lemon. Cover each pudding individually (see pages 180–81) and bake in a roasting tin, with enough boiling water to reach about halfway up their sides, for 40 minutes, at 190°C/375°F/Gas Mark 5.

Walnut and Apple Pudding

A lovely light autumnal steamed pudding.

SERVES 8
use a 2.4 litre/4 pint pudding basin

175g/6oz butter, softened, plus a little extra for greasing
175g/6oz caster sugar
finely grated rind of 1 large orange
3 tbsp cold milk
3 large eggs
175g/6oz self-raising flour
75g/3oz walnuts, chopped
225g/8oz cooking apples, peeled, cored and chopped

Butter the pudding basin well. Cream the butter and sugar together until light and fluffy, then add the orange rind and milk. Beat in one egg at a time, whisking the mixture very well after each addition; do not worry if it curdles. Add about half the flour, then fold in the rest with a metal spoon. Lightly mix in the walnuts and apples.

Put the mixture into the basin, level the surface, then cover and steam (see pages 180–81) for 3 hours. Leave the pudding to stand for 2–3 minutes, before turning out onto a warm dish.

Serve immediately with cream, Custard Sauce (see page 173), Vanilla Ice Cream (see page 148) or natural yogurt.

CHAPTER 5

FOOLS, CUSTARDS AND CREAMS

Gooseberry and Elderflower Fool (and Jelly)
Prune and Brandy Fool
Westminster Fool
Strawberry and Raspberry Fool
Apricot Fool
Damson, Honey and Whisky Fool
Blancmange
Blackcurrant Blancmange
Quince Blancmange
Baked Apple Pudding
Bramley Custard
Burnt Cream
Caramel Cream
Chilled Raspberry Pudding
Mrs Beeton's Quaking Pudding with Blackcurrant Sauce
Chocolate Cream
Strawberry Jelly Cream with Raspberry Sauce
Cold Cream of Tapioca and Redcurrants
Snow and Cream (Iles Flottantes)
Lemon Syllabub

The fool is a very old British dish and is a combination of puréed fruit with custard or cream. This may sound a little humdrum, however the resulting luscious, light cream is perfect to celebrate a summer's day.

The fool's first cousin is that great old British dish, the custard. It began life, according to the OED, *before 1600 as the crustade, which was an open pie containing meat or fruit covered with broth or milk, thickened with eggs, sweetened and seasoned with spices. Over the centuries, however, it has evolved into the universal basic accompaniment to every school boy's pudding and the much loved* Crème Anglaise *to the French.*

At the same time, some of our most elegant puddings – Burnt Cream, Caramel Cream, Snow and Cream – are custard based.

GOOSEBERRY AND ELDERFLOWER FOOL (AND JELLY)

Fools are traditionally made with whipped double cream or custard, or both, but sour cream makes a lovely, light alternative. If fresh elderflowers are not available, add 5 tbsp elderflower cordial (available from good supermarkets or wholefood shops) to the cooled gooseberries.

We much prefer the idea, from E. S. Dallas in *Kettner's Book of the Table* (1877), quoted in Jane Grigson's *Fruit Book*, of just mashing the gooseberries instead of making them completely smooth: 'When the gooseberries are cold, mash them all together. Passing them through a sieve or colander spoils them. The fine natural flavour which resides in the skin no art can replace. The skins must therefore remain unseparated in the general mash.'

SERVES 4–5
use 4–5 glasses

675g/1½lb green gooseberries, topped and tailed
225g/8oz caster sugar
1 handful fresh young elderflowers, thick stems removed and tied in muslin
300ml/½ pint sour cream

Preheat the oven to 180°C/350°F/Gas Mark 4.

Put the gooseberries, sugar and elderflowers into an ovenproof dish, cover and cook in the oven for 30 minutes, shaking the dish once or twice during the cooking time. Take out the elderflowers, strain the fruit, then lightly mash the gooseberries and leave to cool. Fold in the sour cream and divide between the glasses. Serve lightly chilled with Almond, Hazelnut or Walnut Biscuits (see page 175).

VARIATION

For a delicious, fragrant Gooseberry and Elderflower Jelly, keep the gooseberry juice. This quantity should yield about 600ml/1 pint of juice, in which case, add 12g/½oz powdered gelatine to it while it is still hot. Stir the liquid well until all the gelatine has dissolved. Leave the jelly to cool, then chill it and serve it with cream and Almond, Hazelnut or Walnut Biscuits (see page 175).

Prune and Brandy Fool

A luxurious blend of flavours.

SERVES 6
use a 1.2 litre/2 pint serving dish or 6 glasses

225g/8oz prunes, stoned
600ml/1 pint Earl Grey tea
10cm/4in cinnamon stick
strip of orange rind
50g/2oz light muscovado sugar
3 tbsp brandy
300ml/½ pint double cream, lightly whipped
1 large egg white
25g/1oz walnuts, chopped

Preheat the oven to 160°C/325°F/Gas Mark 3.

Put the prunes, tea, cinnamon stick and orange rind into an ovenproof pan, bring to the boil, then cover the pan and bake for 20 minutes. Remove the cinnamon stick and orange rind, then purée the prunes in their juice with the sugar.

Allow the purée to cool, then stir in the brandy and fold in the cream. Whisk the egg white until stiff, but not dry, and fold into the purée with a metal spoon. Transfer to the serving dish or glasses and chill. Scatter the walnuts over the fool just before serving.

Serve chilled, with Walnut Biscuits (see page 175).

Westminster Fool

This is adapted from a recipe in Bernard N. Bessunger's *Recipes of Old England*, although it apparently originates from *The London Cook*, or *The Whole Art of Cookery Made Easy and Familiar*, by William Gelleroy: 'It is not what we would describe as a Fool at all, but more of a Trifle with lots of sherry in it, and would be good served with poached fruit or fresh berries.'

SERVES 6
use a 2.4 litre/4 pint glass or china dish

175g/6oz brioche loaf, thinly sliced
150ml/¼ pint sherry
300ml/½ pint milk
300ml/½ pint single cream
small blade of mace
5 large eggs
25g/1oz caster sugar
1 tbsp rosewater (see page 179)
freshly grated nutmeg

Layer the brioche loaf in the bottom of the serving dish and pour the sherry evenly over the top.

Heat the milk and cream with the mace to just below boiling point, cover the pan and leave to infuse for 30 minutes.

Make a custard with the eggs, sugar and warm milk and cream mixture (see page 173), then take out the mace. Add the rosewater and pour the custard over the brioche. Grate some nutmeg over the custard, allow to cool, then chill.

Serve lightly chilled.

Strawberry and Raspberry Fool

A light, delicately pink summer fool.

SERVES 4–5
use 4–5 glasses

350g/12oz strawberries, hulled
350g/12oz raspberries
75g/3oz caster sugar
1 tbsp orange flower water (see page 179)
300ml/½ pint double cream, lightly whipped

Mix the strawberries, raspberries and sugar together in a bowl. Crush the fruit with the back of a fork and leave to stand for about an hour. Stir in the orange flower water and fold in the cream. Divide the fool between 4–5 glasses and chill.

Serve lightly chilled, with Almond, Hazelnut or Walnut Biscuits (see page 175).

Apricot Fool

Steaming the apricots ensures that they keep all their flavour for this light, fragrant fool.

SERVES 4–5
use 4–5 glasses

450g/1lb fresh apricots
1 large egg
75g/3oz caster sugar
300ml/½ pint double cream, lightly whipped
25g/1oz flaked almonds, toasted (see page 180)

Steam the whole apricots, covered, in a vegetable steamer or metal colander over simmering water until they are just tender, then remove the stones and purée the fruit immediately with the egg and sugar. Leave to cool. Fold the cream into the purée and divide the fool between the glasses. Chill and scatter on the almonds just before serving.

Serve lightly chilled with Macaroons or Shortbread (see pages 176 and 177).

Damson, Honey and Whisky Fool

A lovely way of using damsons.

SERVES 6
use 6 glasses

900g/2lb damsons
strip of orange rind
8 generous tbsp honey
3 tbsp whisky
300ml/½ pint double cream, lightly whipped
25g/1oz porridge oats, toasted

Preheat the oven to 160°C/325°F/Gas Mark 3.

Put the damsons and orange rind into an ovenproof dish and cook for about 20 minutes until the damsons are just tender. Take out the orange rind and press the fruit through a fairly coarse sieve. Stir in the honey, then leave the purée to cool.

Add the whisky and fold in the cream. Divide the fool between 6 glasses. Chill, sprinkling with toasted porridge oats just before serving.

Serve lightly chilled, with Almond, Hazelnut or Walnut Biscuits (see page 175).

BLANCMANGE

Dismiss any memories of school blancmange and try this luxurious, soothing version flavoured with bay leaves, rosewater and honey, inspired by a recipe in Christiana Awdry's *Household Book*, which was written in the eighteenth century. It has recently been republished, edited and annotated by Margaret Jensen.

SERVES 6

use a 1.2 litre/2 pint jelly mould, glass or china dish or 6 glasses

600ml/1 pint cold milk
300ml/½ pint double cream
3 generous tbsp honey
3 bay leaves, broken in half
11.7g/½oz powdered gelatine (see page 179)
3 tbsp rosewater

Stir the milk, cream and honey together with the bay leaves in a saucepan. Bring to boiling point, remove from the heat, cover the saucepan and leave to infuse for 30 minutes.

Remove the bay leaves from the warm milk mixture and sprinkle on the gelatine. Stir the mixture well until the gelatine has completely dissolved. Add the rosewater and pour the blancmange into the mould (see page 181). Leave to cool, then chill.

Serve chilled, with or without fresh summer berries or a fruit sauce.

Blackcurrant Blancmange

This velvety blancmange has a glorious, creamy blackcurrant flavour. The idea for it comes from Eliza Acton's *Modern Cookery for Private Families*, first published in 1845: 'Black currants would, we think, make an agreeable variety of blancmange for persons who like their peculiar flavour, but we have not tried them.'

SERVES 6
use a 1.2 litre/2 pint jelly mould, glass or china dish

450g/1lb blackcurrants, stripped from the stalk
225g/8oz caster sugar
3 tbsp cold water
11.7g/½oz powdered gelatine (see page 179)
300ml/½ pint double cream
450ml/¾ pint cold milk

Put the blackcurrants and sugar into a heavy-based saucepan and heat gently until the sugar has dissolved, then simmer for 10 minutes. Leave to cool slightly, then purée.

Heat the water without letting it boil, then add the gelatine and stir to dissolve. Stir the dissolved gelatine, cream and milk into the blackcurrant purée and pour the mixture into the jelly mould (see page 181) or dish. Leave the blancmange to cool, then chill.

Serve chilled, with Almond, Hazelnut or Walnut Biscuits (see page 175).

QUINCE BLANCMANGE

Quinces have a unique, mellow flavour, and although they are only available for a short time during the autumn, this recipe is well worth trying. It is from Eliza Acton's *Modern Cookery for Private Families*, first published in 1845, and is subtitled 'Delicious'. She also says: 'This if carefully made, and with ripe quinces, is one of the most richly-flavoured preparations of fruit that we have ever tasted; and the receipt, we may venture to say will be altogether new to the reader.'

Chop the whole quinces, including the pips, core and skin, straight into a bowl of water with a little lemon juice added, to stop them from turning brown. Strain the fruit before cooking.

SERVES 4

use a 600ml/1 pint jelly mould or glass or china dish, 4 glasses or 4 individual 75g/6fl oz pudding basins

450g/1lb ripe quinces, chopped (see above)
600ml/1 pint cold water
50g/2oz caster sugar
11.7g/½oz powdered gelatine (see page 179)
150ml/¼ pint double cream

Put the quinces into a saucepan with the water, cover and simmer for about 30 minutes, then leave them in their juice overnight. Strain the quinces through a piece of muslin; leave to drip until all the juice has been extracted, but do not squeeze the fruit. This should yield about 375–400ml/13–14fl oz of juice.

Put the quince juice and sugar into a saucepan and heat gently until the sugar has dissolved, then remove from the heat. Add the gelatine and stir until dissolved. Leave the mixture until it is just cool, then mix in the cream. Pour the blancmange into the jelly mould or basins (see page 181), dish or glasses, then chill.

Serve chilled, turned out of the mould or basins or spooned from the dish or glasses, with Macaroons or Shortbread (see pages 176 and 177).

Baked Apple Pudding

This is based on one of Mrs Beeton's recipes. She suggests either leaving the skins on the halved apples *or* using peeled, sliced apples in the batter, in which case sprinkle the raisins over them.

SERVES 6
use a 3 litre/5 pint shallow ovenproof dish

3 tbsp plain white flour
3 medium eggs
600ml/1 pint cold milk
3 tbsp rum
50g/2oz raisins
900g/2lb small eating apples, cut in half and cored (see above)
25g/1oz butter, plus a little extra for greasing
freshly grated nutmeg
about 50g/2oz caster sugar

Preheat the oven to 180°C/350°F/Gas Mark 4 and butter the dish well.

Mix together the flour and eggs, then gradually add the milk to make a smooth batter. Stir in the rum.

Put the raisins into the centre of the apple halves and arrange them, cut side down, in the dish. Pour over the batter, dot the surface with butter and grate some nutmeg on top. Bake the pudding for 1 hour, then sprinkle thickly with the sugar.

Serve immediately, with or without cream.

Bramley Custard

This is a recipe based on one of Mrs Beeton's and is a gentle, very British apple pudding.

SERVES 6
use a 2.4 litre/4 pint ovenproof dish or 6 large ramekins 80mm/3¼in in diameter and 45mm/1¾in high

For the fruit

900g/2lb Bramley apples, peeled, cored and thinly sliced
3 generous tbsp honey
finely grated rind of ½ lemon

For the custard

6 medium egg yolks
50g/2oz caster sugar
600ml/1 pint cold milk

For the meringue

6 medium egg whites
25g/1oz caster sugar

Preheat the oven to 150°C/300°F/Gas Mark 2.

Put the apples, honey and lemon rind (peel) into a heavy-based saucepan and cook over a very low heat until the apples are just tender. Purée the apples and put them into the dish or ramekins.

Make the custard with the egg yolks, sugar and milk (see page 173) and pour it over the apple purée.

Whisk the egg whites until stiff, but not dry, then fold in the sugar with a metal spoon. Pile the meringue over the custard, sealing it to the edge of the dish, and bake for 30 minutes until the meringue is golden brown.

Serve warm or cold, with or without cream or natural yogurt.

BURNT CREAM (CRÈME BRÛLÉE)

Recipes for Burnt Cream appear in many old British cookery books, including *The London Art of Cookery* by John Farley (1789). However, we now tend to think of the dish as French and usually call it *Crème Brûlée*. The caramel was traditionally made using a salamander, which according to the *Oxford English Dictionary* is a circular iron plate that is heated and placed over a pudding to brown it. Nowadays, many restaurants use a blowlamp. A domestic grill, turned up to the maximum temperature, is the most practical alternative, but will not provide the same intensity of heat. The grilled sugar caramelises, but will only form a thin, fairly crisp, uneven surface over the cream.

For a completely smooth finish, the caramel must be made in a saucepan and poured over the cream. Melt 175g/6oz caster sugar with 1 tbsp cold water in a heavy-based saucepan, shaking it from time to time, without stirring. When the caramel is dark golden, put the base of the saucepan into cold water for a moment or two, then pour the caramel quickly over the chilled custard.

Do not make the caramel more than a few hours before serving the Burnt Cream otherwise it will dissolve.

SERVES 6

use a 900ml/1½ pint shallow ovenproof dish or 6 small ramekins 75mm/3in in diameter and 40mm/1½ high

For the custard

600ml/1 pint double cream
strip of lemon rind
10cm/4in cinnamon stick
4 medium egg yolks
50g/2oz caster sugar

For the caramel

6 tsp caster sugar

Put the cream, lemon rind and cinnamon stick into a heavy-based saucepan, bring the cream to boiling point, then remove the saucepan from the heat. Cover the pan and leave the contents to infuse for 30 minutes.

Make a custard with the cream, lemon rind, cinnamon, egg yolks and sugar (see page 173), then take out the lemon rind and cinnamon stick and pour the custard into the dish or ramekins. Leave to cool, then chill overnight.

About 2 hours before serving preheat the grill to maximum temperature. To make the caramel, sprinkle the sugar evenly over the custard and put it as near as possible under the grill until it has turned golden brown and caramelised.

Serve lightly chilled.

Caramel Cream

Despite its reputation, Caramel Cream is deceptively easy to make. Turn it onto a deep plate to catch the caramel which will have dissolved into a syrup.

Ideally, the ovenproof dish, in which the Caramel Cream is made, should measure about 16cm/6½in in diameter and have sides about 85mm/3½in high.

SERVES 6
use a 1.5 litre/2½ pint ovenproof dish

For the caramel

100g/4oz caster sugar

For the custard

6 medium eggs
50g/2oz caster sugar
900ml/1½ pints cold milk

Preheat the oven to 160°C/325°F/Gas Mark 3.

Put the sugar for the caramel into a heavy-based frying pan. Dissolve it over medium heat, stirring it continuously with a wooden spoon. The sugar will initially have a sticky consistency, but after a few minutes it will dissolve and form a thickish golden-brown syrup. Pour the syrup into the dish and quickly tip it from side to side to spread the caramel over the base.

Beat the eggs and sugar together in a large bowl. Warm the milk to blood heat, then pour it over the eggs and sugar, stirring well. Pour the mixture over the caramel and place the dish in a roasting tin with enough boiling water to reach about halfway up its sides.

Cook for 1 hour or until the tip of a knife inserted in the centre comes out clean. Leave to cool, then chill before loosening the sides and turn out onto a deep plate.

Serve lightly chilled and cut into wedges, with cream.

VARIATION

To make 4 individual Caramel Creams in large ramekins 80mm/3¼in in diameter and 45mm/1¾in high, use 75g/3oz caster (superfine) sugar for the caramel and half the above quantity for the custard. Cook the individual Caramel Creams for 40 minutes in a roasting tin as above.

CHILLED RASPBERRY PUDDING

From *The English Cookery Book*, edited by J. A. Walsh and published in 1858. A delectable cold baked custard with raspberries in it.

SERVES 4–6
use a 1.2 litre/2 pint ovenproof dish

450g/1lb raspberries
100g/4oz caster sugar
6 medium eggs
600ml/1 pint cold milk

Mix the raspberries and half the sugar together gently in the ovenproof dish and leave at room temperature for about 1 hour.

Preheat the oven to 180°C/350°F/Gas Mark 4.

Lightly beat the eggs with the rest of the sugar, then add the milk and pour the mixture over the raspberries. Bake the pudding for 45 minutes, then leave to cool before chilling.

Serve lightly chilled with or without cream.

Mrs Beeton's Quaking Pudding with Blackcurrant Sauce

We were intrigued by the name of this pudding which appears in many old cookery books. It is an extremely rich, creamy dish, and tastes spectacular with Blackcurrant Sauce. It looks old fashioned and inviting made as a single pudding, but is difficult to spoon and will probably only serve about 8 people. However, turned out of small ramekins, the following quantity is enough for 12.

SERVES 8–12
use a 1.5 litre/2½ pint pudding basin

For the pudding

butter for greasing
1.2 litre/2 pints double cream
100g/4oz caster sugar
1½ tbsp plain white flour
freshly grated nutmeg
4 medium eggs

For the sauce

450g/1lb blackcurrants, stripped from the stalk
165g/5½oz caster sugar

Butter the pudding basin well. Bring the cream to boiling point, then leave to cool a little. Mix the sugar with the flour and nutmeg in a mixing bowl, then lightly beat in the eggs. Stir the cream into the egg mixture, then pour into the pudding basin. Cover and steam the pudding (see pages 180–82) for 30 minutes.

To make the sauce, put the blackcurrants and sugar into a saucepan, bring slowly to the boil and simmer for 3–4 minutes, stirring all the time. Purée the sauce. Turn out the Quaking Pudding onto a deep plate and pour the sauce over. Serve immediately.

VARIATION

To make individual puddings, use twelve small ramekins 75mm/3in in diameter and 40mm/1½in high and butter them well. Divide the mixture between them and grate the nutmeg on top of each pudding just before cooking instead of mixing it in. Cover each ramekin with a piece of buttered, pleated greaseproof paper, followed by a piece of pleated foil, then tie in place with string (see diagram on page 181). Place the puddings in a roasting tin with enough boiling water to reach about halfway up their sides, and cook for 30 minutes at 180°C/350°F/Gas Mark 4. Leave to stand for 1–2 minutes, then turn out onto warm plates and serve hot with Blackcurrant Sauce.

Chocolate Cream

A very smooth, very chocolaty pudding from Christiana Awdry's *Household Book*, first written in the eighteenth century.

SERVES 6

use a 1.2 litre/2 pint dish, 6 glasses or 6 small ramekins 75mm/3in in diameter and 40mm/1½in high

100g/4oz bitter chocolate
150ml/¼ pint cold water
25g/1oz caster sugar
600ml/1 pint double cream
2 large eggs, beaten

Break the chocolate into pieces and put it in a saucepan with the water and sugar. Bring to the boil, then simmer, whisking with a balloon whisk, until the chocolate has melted and the sugar dissolved. Add the cream and eggs and bring back to the boil, whisking continually.

Leave the mixture to cool, whisking it now and then to prevent a skin forming, then pour into a dish, glasses or ramekins, and chill.

Serve chilled, with cream and Almond, Hazelnut or Walnut Biscuits (see page 175).

Strawberry Jelly Cream with Raspberry Sauce

This smooth jelly cream, which is very similar to a blancmange, really accentuates the full flavour of fresh summer strawberries and is adapted from one of Eliza Acton's recipes in *Modern Cookery for Private Families*, first published in 1845.

SERVES 12

use a 2.1 litre/3½ pint jelly mould, or glass or china dish, 12 glasses or 12 individual 75ml/6fl oz pudding basins

For the jelly cream

675g/1½lb strawberries, hulled
225g/8oz caster sugar
600ml/1 pint cold milk
23.4g/1oz powdered gelatine (see page 179)
450g/¾ pint double cream • 3 tbsp lemon juice

For the sauce

674g/1½lb raspberries
175g/6oz caster sugar
75ml/3fl oz orange juice

Crush the strawberries with the back of a spoon and stir in the sugar. Leave to stand for 3–4 hours, then purée.

Heat the milk to just below boiling point, turn off the heat, sprinkle on the gelatine and stir well until the gelatine has completely dissolved. Mix in the cream, strawberry purée and lemon juice. Pour the mixture into the jelly mould or basins (see page 181), dish or glasses, leave the jelly cream to cool, then chill for several hours.

To make the raspberry sauce, purée the raspberries with the sugar and add the orange juice. Serve lightly chilled, with the sauce and Macaroons or Shortbread (see pages 176 and 177).

Cold Cream of Tapioca and Redcurrants

It's difficult not to associate tapioca with awful school dinners and instantly think of frogspawn. However, this recipe adapted from *The Gentle Art of Cookery* by Mrs C. F. Leyel and Miss Olga Hartley, first published in 1925, is a divine, light pudding with a superb contrast of flavours and tastes. The original recipe suggests serving the tapioca and redcurrants in separate glass dishes, but we prefer to put the fruit into 6 tall glasses, with the tapioca on top of it.

According to Mrs Beeton, tapioca is the 'produce of the pith of the cassava-tree, made in the East Indies and Brazil' and is highly nutritious.

SERVES 6
use 6 glasses

For the tapioca

1.2 litres/2 pints cold milk
vanilla pod
50g/2oz tapioca
50g/2oz caster sugar
ground cinnamon for dusting

For the fruit

350g/12oz redcurrants, stripped from the stalk
175g/6oz caster sugar

Put the milk, vanilla pod, tapioca and sugar into a saucepan, bring slowly to the boil, then simmer for about 20 minutes, stirring fairly frequently, until the tapioca has swollen and become completely transparent. Leave the tapioca to cool completely.

Meanwhile, put the redcurrants with the sugar into a saucepan and bring very slowly to the boil, stirring once. Take the fruit off the heat and leave to cool. Divide the fruit between 6 glasses and spoon the tapioca on top. Chill, then dust the surface with a little ground cinnamon. Serve chilled, with Almond, Hazelnut or Walnut Biscuits (see page 175).

Snow and Cream (Iles Flottantes)

Elizabeth Raffald, in *The Experienced English Housekeeper*, first published in 1805, calls this dish Snow and Cream, although it is now more commonly known as Floating Islands or Iles Flottantes. This was certainly a popular pudding in England during the 1930s, though not so fashionable now. It's hard to pinpoint where the recipe originated and it is a typical example of culinary ideas crossing the Channel freely in both directions.

We struggled desperately to find a way of getting the meringues to cook successfully without flopping down afterwards and only discovered this method at the last moment before giving up completely. The praline can be stored for several weeks in an airtight container.

SERVES 6
use a large shallow dish or 6 deep individual plates

For the custard

300ml/½ pint single cream
300ml/½ pint cold milk
vanilla pod
25g/1oz caster sugar
4 medium egg yolks

For the meringue islands

4 medium egg whites
50g/2oz caster sugar

For the praline

oil for greasing
50g/2oz sugar
50g/2oz whole unblanched almonds

Make the custard with the cream, milk, vanilla pod, sugar and egg yolks (see page 173). Chill.

To make the meringue islands, whisk the egg whites until stiff, but not dry. Whisk in about half of the sugar, then fold in the rest with a metal spoon. Meanwhile, bring a large, deep pan of water to the boil, then reduce the heat to maintain a gentle simmer. Form tablespoonfuls of the meringue into egg shapes and place a few at a time, well spaced out, on the water. Cook for 3 minutes on each side, then use a perforated spoon to transfer the meringues onto a clean tea towel or absorbent kitchen paper. Leave to cool.

To make the praline, lightly oil a baking sheet. Put the sugar and almonds into a heavy-based saucepan and stir over a medium heat until the sugar has melted and turned golden brown. Pour the mixture onto the oiled baking sheet and leave it to harden. Finely chop the caramelised almonds or crush with a rolling pin.

Cover the base of the dish or plates with the chilled custard. Arrange the meringues on top, then sprinkle with the praline. Serve immediately.

Lemon Syllabub

Dorothy Hartley in *Food for England* (1954) says of Syllabub: '(spelt also Sillabub, Sillebub etc.) Sill was part of the Champagne country from which the wine Sill or Sille took its name, Bub was the common Elizabethan slang name for a bubbling drink, later, by association, a belly, and a syllabub was made by mixing the wine Sille with frothing cream – to make a Sille Bub.' The following recipe is based on one from *The Compleat Housewife* by Eliza Smith, first published in 1758.

SERVES 6–8
use 6–8 wine glasses

300ml/½ pint double cream
50g/2oz caster sugar
150ml/¼ pint sweet white wine
finely grated rind of ½ lemon • 3 tbsp lemon juice

Mix all the ingredients together in a large bowl, then whisk until thick and light. Put the syllabub into 6–8 glasses and chill for 5–6 hours or overnight. Serve chilled, with Almond, Hazelnut or Walnut Biscuits (see page 175).

CHAPTER 6

JELLIES, TRIFLES, JUNKETS AND PANCAKES

Orange Jelly
Spiced Red Wine Jelly
Strawberry Jelly
Blackberry and Apple Jelly
Chocolate Rum Trifle with Cherries (or Pears)
Gooseberry Trifle
Sherry Trifle with Raspberries
Devonshire Junket
Elderflower Junket
Coffee Junket
Ale Pancakes in a Pile
Kaiserschmarren
Pancakes with Lemon
Poor Knights of Windsor
Rhubarb Fritters
Spiced Apple Pancake

This is a group of British puddings, all of which have been traditionally decried. In fact they are delicious and deserve their present renaissance.

A sparkling jelly made from fresh fruit is a grievously underrated British pudding and a delight to eat on a summer's day. It is also surprisingly simple to prepare.

Junket has all but disappeared from our kitchens today, however its delicate simplicity fits very well with current taste. It is an extremely light, soothing pudding made primarily of milk and first cousin to fromage frais or a mild natural yogurt. Junket is also incredibly easy to make and quite delicious when delicately flavoured with elderflowers, coffee or brandy.

It has always been a particular delight to us to see how our French cousins rhapsodise about the trifle – a dish which after all started life as a handy way of using up unpromising leftovers like stale cake. Of course, a liberal admixture of sherry greatly multiplies its attraction. Oliver Wendell Holmes summed it up in 1860: 'That most wonderful object of domestic art called trifle . . . with its charming confusion of cream and cake and almonds and jam and jelly and wine and cinnamon and froth.'

Pancakes are not a uniquely British pudding by any means and have been adopted by every culture. The current traditionally British, rather frugal version is mainly eaten on Shrove Tuesday. However, our ancestors enjoyed more extravagant varieties made with cream, ale, sherry and spices.

Orange Jelly

A very fresh tasting jelly with a hint of sherry, traditionally served in empty orange shells. Four large oranges should yield about 600ml/1 pint orange juice.

SERVES 4–6
use a 900ml/1½ pint jelly mould or glass dish or 4–6 glasses

thinly pared rind of 1 orange
50ml/2fl oz sherry
150ml/¼ pint cold water
100g/4oz granulated sugar
11.7g/½oz powdered gelatine (see page 179)
600ml/1 pint orange juice
3 tbsp lemon juice

Soak the orange rind in the sherry for 1 hour.

Bring the water to boiling point, add the sugar and stir until dissolved. Turn off the heat, sprinkle the gelatine onto the syrup and stir again until the gelatine has completely dissolved.

Take the orange peel out of the sherry, then mix the sherry and orange and lemon juice into the gelatine syrup. Leave to cool, then pour the liquid into the mould (see page 181), dish or glasses and chill the jelly for several hours.

Serve chilled, with cream or Vanilla Ice Cream (see page 148) and Macaroons or Shortbread (see pages 176 and 177).

Spiced Red Wine Jelly

A mellow jelly with the flavour of mulled wine.

SERVES 6

use a 1.5 litre/2½ pint jelly mould, glass dish or 6 glasses

600ml/1 pint red wine
10cm/4in cinnamon stick
1 small blade mace
2 whole cloves
pared rind of ½ lemon
225g/8oz caster sugar
23.4g/1oz powdered gelatine (see page 179)
600ml/1 pint cold water
2 tbsp brandy
1 tbsp lemon juice

Put the wine, cinnamon stick, blade of mace, cloves, lemon rind and sugar into a saucepan. Bring the mixture to the boil, stir, then remove the saucepan from the heat, cover and leave to infuse for 30 minutes.

Strain the warm wine mixture, sprinkle on the gelatine and stir well until the gelatine has completely dissolved. Add the water, brandy and lemon juice, then pour the jelly into the mould (see page 181), dish or glasses and chill.

Serve chilled, with cream or Vanilla Ice Cream (see page 148) and Macaroons or Shortbread (see pages 176 and 177).

Strawberry Jelly

This recipe can be multiplied to serve more people and is a lovely way to serve strawberries for a party without worrying whether they are at their best (see also Strawberry Jelly Cream with Raspberry Sauce).

SERVES 2–3
use a 600ml/1 pint jelly mould, glass dish or 2–3 glasses

450g/1lb strawberries, hulled and thickly sliced, plus 2–3 extra
100g/4oz caster sugar
11.7g/½oz powdered gelatine (see page 179)
50ml/2fl oz cold water
125ml/4fl oz sweet white wine

Preheat the oven to 140°C/275°F/Gas Mark 1.

Put the strawberries and sugar into an ovenproof dish, cover and cook in the oven for 1 hour. Strain the juice into a measuring jug (there should be about 300ml/½ pint) and whisk the gelatine into the hot liquid, mixing it in well until the gelatine has completely dissolved.

Stir in the water and wine and pour the jelly into the mould (see page 181), dish or glasses. Slice the extra strawberries thinly and drop them into the jelly. Leave to cool then chill.

Serve chilled, with cream or Vanilla Ice Cream (see page 148) and Macaroons or Shortbread (see pages 176 and 177).

Blackberry and Apple Jelly

From *The Gentle Art of Cookery* by Mrs C. F. Leyel and Miss Olga Hartley, first published in 1925. This is a solid fruit jelly rather than a clear one, with an intensified blackberry and apple flavour.

SERVES 4–5
use a 1.2 litre/2 pint jelly mould, glass or china dish or 4–5 glasses

450g/1lb blackberries
450g/1lb cooking apples, peeled, cored and sliced
175g/6oz caster sugar
2 whole cloves, tied in muslin
strip of lemon rind
3 tbsp cold water
11.7g/½oz powdered gelatine (see page 179)

Put the blackberries, apples, sugar, cloves and lemon rind in a saucepan and cook over a low heat until the fruit is just tender. Remove the cloves and lemon rind and purée the fruit. Heat the water, but do not let it boil, then sprinkle on the gelatine and stir until the gelatine has completely dissolved. Mix the gelatine mixture well into the warm purée, then leave to cool. Pour the fruit into the mould (see page 181), dish or glasses, then chill.

Serve chilled, with cream, Vanilla Ice Cream (see page 148) or natural yogurt and Macaroons or Shortbread (see pages 176 and 177).

Chocolate Rum Trifle with Cherries (or Pears)

A serious chocolate pudding. Make the trifle at least 24 hours before serving it.

SERVES 6

use a 2.3 litre/4 pint glass or china dish

225g/8oz chocolate sponge cake
50g/2oz ratafia biscuits (see page 179)
75ml/3fl oz orange juice
50ml/2fl oz rum
225g/8oz cherries, stalks removed and stoned (or pears, see below)
100g/4oz bitter chocolate, broken into pieces, plus a little extra for grating
600ml/1 pint cold milk
5 large eggs
25g/1oz caster sugar
300ml/½ pint double cream, lightly whipped

Put the cake and ratafia biscuits in the bottom of the dish. Mix the orange juice and rum together and pour evenly over the cake and biscuits. Scatter the cherries on top and gently level it all with the back of a fork.

Slowly melt the chocolate in the milk, then make a custard (see page 173) with the eggs, sugar and chocolate milk. Pour the chocolate custard over the cherries.

When the custard is cold, cover it with a layer of cream. If the cream does not cover the custard completely, make a marble pattern with the chocolate custard and the cream using the prongs of a fork. Grate some chocolate over the cream and chill.

Serve lightly chilled.

VARIATION

As an alternative use half the quantity of the Pears in Ginger Wine recipe on page 163 instead of the cherries. Slice the pears when they are cooked, reduce the syrup to about 150ml/¼ pint and use it instead of the orange juice and rum.

Gooseberry Trifle

This is a delectable combination of textures and flavours, rather like a fool served in layers, and is one of Mrs Beeton's recipes.

SERVES 6
use a 2.4 litre/4 pint glass or china dish

For the fruit

625g/1¾lb gooseberries, topped and tailed
100g/4oz caster sugar

For the custard and cream

600ml/1 pint cold milk
pared rind of ½ lemon
75g/3oz caster sugar
5 medium eggs
1 tbsp brandy
300ml/½ pint double cream, lightly whipped
50g/2oz macaroons, crushed or ratafia biscuits (see page 179)

Preheat the oven to 160°C/325°F/Gas Mark 3.

Put the gooseberries and sugar into an ovenproof dish, cook in the oven for 30 minutes, then crush lightly with a fork. Leave the gooseberries to cool, then put them into the dish.

Bring the milk to boiling point with the lemon rind, then make a custard with the warm milk, sugar and eggs (see page 173). Take the lemon rind out of the custard and leave to cool, stirring occasionally. Add the brandy and pour over the gooseberries.

Cover the custard with a layer of cream and chill. Scatter the crushed macaroon or ratafia biscuits over the trifle just before serving.

Serve lightly chilled.

Sherry Trifle with Raspberries

There is no standard recipe for a trifle today because every family, cook, caterer or chef has his or her own version, with or without fruit, cake, jam or alcohol, but almost always including custard and cream.

Trifles are best eaten at least 24 hours after they are made.

SERVES 6
use a 2.4 litre/4 pint glass or china dish

about 50g/2oz raspberry jam
225g/8oz sponge cake, sliced
50g/2oz ratafia biscuits (see page 179)
150ml/¼ pint sherry
175g/6oz raspberries
5 large eggs
25g/1oz caster sugar
600ml/1 pint cold milk
vanilla pod
300ml/½ pint double cream, lightly whipped
25g/1oz flaked almonds, toasted (see page 180)

Spread the jam onto the slices of cake and arrange in the bottom of the dish with the ratafia biscuits. Pour the sherry as evenly as possible over the cake and biscuits, scatter the raspberries on top, then gently level it all with the back of a fork.

Make the custard with the eggs, sugar, milk and vanilla pod as described on page 173. Take out the vanilla pod and pour the custard over the raspberries. Leave the custard to cool.

When the custard is cold, cover with a layer of cream and chill. Scatter the surface of the trifle with the almonds just before serving it.

Serve lightly chilled.

Devonshire Junket

As Florence White says in *Good Things in England*, first published in 1932: 'Junket is not a thing that improves by keeping after being once cut, as the whey then runs out of it. Thus if the quantity likely to be eaten is doubtful, it is a good plan after mixing the milk with the rennet to pour it at once to set in little cups or glasses.' It should not be kept in any case for much more than 24 hours.

Whole or creamy milk is usually recommended for junket, but semi-skimmed milk can be used. This junket has been traced back to the seventeenth century. It is often served with a layer of clotted cream spread on top of it.

SERVES 6

use 6 large ramekins 80mm/3¼in in diameter and 45mm/1¾in high

1.2 litre/2 pints cold milk
25g/1oz caster sugar
4 tbsp brandy or rum
4 tsp (2 dessertspoon) liquid rennet (see page 179)
freshly grated nutmeg

Put the milk, sugar and brandy into a saucepan and warm slowly to 98.4°C or blood heat. Add the rennet and stir the mixture once. Pour the junket into the ramekins and grate over a little nutmeg. Leave the junket to cool at room temperature, then chill.

Serve chilled, with or without cream.

Elderflower Junket

A cool delicate junket. The crystallised violet petals look very pretty on it, but can only be put on at the last minute because they start turning it purple after about an hour.

SERVES 3

use 3 large ramekins 80mm/3¼in in diameter and 45mm/1¾in high

a handful of fresh young elderflowers, thick stems removed
600ml/1 pint cold milk
1 tbsp caster sugar
2 tsp (1 dessertspoonful) liquid rennet (see page 179)
crystallised violet petals

Tie the elderflowers in a piece of muslin and place in a saucepan with the milk and sugar. Slowly bring to just below boiling point, stir, then remove from the heat. Cover and leave to infuse until the milk cools to 98.4°C or blood heat.

Take out the elderflowers, add the rennet, stir the mixture once and pour the junket into the ramekins. Leave the junket to cool at room temperature, then chill.

Serve chilled and decorated *at the last minute* with some crystallised violets.

Coffee Junket

This junket has an unusual and subtle flavour.

SERVES 3
use 3 large ramekins 80mm/3¼in in diameter and 45mm/1¾in high

600ml/1 pint cold milk
1 tbsp caster sugar
2 tbsp very strong black coffee
2 tsp (1 dessertspoonful) liquid rennet (see page 179)
about 25g/1oz bitter chocolate

Put the milk, sugar and coffee into a saucepan and warm slowly to 98.4°C or blood heat. Add the rennet, stir the mixture once and pour the junket into the ramekins. Leave to cool at room temperature, then chill.

Serve chilled, with a little chocolate grated over at the last minute.

Ale Pancakes in a Pile

This is a recipe from Elinor Fettiplace's *Receipt Book*, originally published in 1604, and was apparently a favourite dish of Pepys. The pancakes are layered with butter and cinnamon sugar, then cut into wedges and served hot with a sherry sauce.

SERVES 5
use a frying pan about 15cm/6in in diameter

For the pancakes

225g/8oz plain white flour
½ tsp ground ginger
freshly grated nutmeg
generous pinch of ground cloves
pinch of salt
2 medium eggs
350ml/12fl oz light ale
3 tbsp sherry
sunflower oil

For the filling

50g/2oz light muscovado sugar
1 tsp ground cinnamon
25g/1oz butter, melted

For the sauce

50g/2oz butter
50g/2oz dark muscovado sugar
3 tbsp sherry
finely grated rind of ½ orange

Heat the oven to its lowest temperature. To make the pancakes, either put the flour, spices, salt, eggs, ale and sherry in a food processor and process for a few seconds to make a smooth batter, or roughly mix the eggs into the flour and spices with a wooden spoon, then gradually add the liquid to make a smooth batter.

Put about 3mm/1/8in of oil into the frying pan to cover the base well and heat until the oil starts to smoke. Pour the excess oil into a ramekin and wipe the pan with a piece of absorbent kitchen paper. Spoon a ladleful (see page 128) of batter into the centre of the pan and immediately tip the pan from side to side to cover the surface with it. Leave the pancake over fairly high heat for a moment or two until the underside is golden brown, then loosen the pancake with a spatula and flip it over. Cook the second side for a few moments, then slide the pancake onto a warm plate.

Before cooking each subsequent pancake, tip the oil in the ramekin back into the pan, re-heat it, recoating the base, then tip the oil out and wipe the pan with absorbent kitchen paper again.

Mix together the light muscovado sugar and the cinnamon. Brush each pancake with a little melted butter, sprinkle over some of the cinnamon sugar and arrange the pancakes in a pile on a warm plate. Keep them hot in a very low oven covered loosely with foil.

To make the sauce, melt the butter and dark muscovado sugar together in a saucepan, stirring continuously, until the sugar has dissolved. Add the sherry and the orange rind.

Serve the pancakes hot, cut into wedges like a cake and drizzled with some of the hot sherry sauce.

KAISERSCHMARREN

This is a well-known *Austrian* pudding. It is thought to have been a favourite of the Emperor Francis Josef, hence the name which literally means 'Emperor's folly'. It's a glorified pancake, sprinkled with raisins and broken into pieces with a fork . . . it is also our publisher Colin Webb's favourite pudding of all and we include it especially for him. However, we were amazed to discover a seventeenth-century British recipe for Spiced Apple Pancake (see page 133) which is very similar.

SERVES 2–3
use a frying pan approximately 24cm/9½in in diameter

100g/4oz plain white flour
pinch of salt
25g/1oz caster sugar
2 large egg yolks
225ml/8fl oz cold milk
25g/1oz butter, melted
25g/1oz raisins
2 large egg whites
25g/1oz butter for frying
1 tbsp granulated or vanilla sugar for sprinkling

Mix the flour, salt and sugar together in a large bowl and stir in the egg yolks. Gradually add the milk to make a smooth batter. Add the melted butter and raisins. Whisk the egg whites until stiff, but not dry, and fold them in with a metal spoon.

Heat the butter in the frying pan until it is as hot as possible without allowing it to brown. Pour the batter into the pan and cook for 2–3 minutes until the underside is golden brown. Flip the pancake over (it doesn't matter if it breaks) and cook for another couple of minutes.

Remove the frying pan from the heat and break the pancake up roughly with two forks. Pile the pancake pieces onto a warm shallow dish and sprinkle over the sugar.

Serve immediately.

Pancakes with Lemon

Pancake making has become a bit of an art in our households due to the passion that Max – our son and grandson – has for them. Pancakes for breakfast are a weekend treat and cooking them, bleary eyed, first thing in the morning has to be a military operation. Certain indispensable pieces of kitchen equipment have to be lined up by the cooker: 1) a 24cm/9½in heavy frying pan; 2) a small ladle that holds 3 tbsp of liquid; 3) a short, wide spatula; 4) a ramekin; 5) absorbent kitchen paper; 6) a warm plate. These can of course be substituted with anything similar, but it's worth having them ready.

Pancakes are best eaten very hot, straight from the pan, but may be kept warm for a short time, piled up, in a cool oven or on a plate over a pan of simmering water covered lightly with foil. They can also be stored for longer in the fridge or freezer, in which case they need to be wrapped in foil with a piece of greaseproof paper between each pancake. Reheat them in a cool oven or over water.

MAKES ABOUT 7 PANCAKES
use a 24cm/9½in heavy frying pan

100g/4oz plain white flour
1 large egg
300ml/½ pint cold milk
sunflower oil
about 3 tbsp lemon juice
about 3 tbsp caster sugar

Either put the flour, egg and milk into a food processor and process for a few seconds to make a smooth batter, or roughly mix the egg into the flour with a wooden spoon, then gradually add the milk to make a smooth batter.

Put about 3mm/⅛in of oil into the frying pan to cover the base well and heat until the oil starts to smoke. Pour the excess oil into the ramekin and wipe the pan with a piece of absorbent kitchen paper. Spoon a ladleful of batter into the centre of the pan and immediately tip the pan from side to side to spread out the batter. Leave the pancake over fairly high heat for a moment or two until the underside is golden brown, then loosen it with the spatula and flip it over. Cook the second side for a few moments, then slide the pancake onto a warm plate.

Before cooking each subsequent pancake, tip the oil in the ramekin back into the pan, re-heat it, recoating the base, then tip the oil out and wipe the pan with absorbent kitchen paper again.

To serve, drizzle about a teaspoonful of lemon juice onto each pancake, roll up the pancakes, then sprinkle with sugar.

Poor Knights of Windsor

A sophisticated version of Eggy Bread from medieval times, originally called Payn-pur-dew (Pain Perdu). This dish is often made with stale bread. However, pieces of brioche or similar bread transform it into something quite special, to be eaten either on its own or with fresh berries, ice cream, fruit sauce or a mixture of all three.

To clarify butter, melt it then simmer until the foaming stops. Pour the butter into a bowl and leave it to solidify. Scrape away the light top layer and discard any liquid underneath the butter.

SERVES 6

3 tbsp caster sugar
1 tsp ground cinnamon
3 large egg yolks, lightly beaten
about 1 tbsp sherry per slice of brioche loaf
9 thick slices brioche loaf, cut in half
100g/4oz clarified butter (see above)

Mix together the sugar and cinnamon and set aside. Put the egg yolks and sherry into separate shallow dishes. Dip the pieces of brioche first into the sherry, and then into the egg yolks. Heat the butter in a frying pan until very hot and fry the brioche quickly on both sides until golden brown.

Serve immediately, sprinkled with the cinnamon sugar.

Rhubarb Fritters

A novel recipe from Eliza Acton's *Modern Cookery for Private Families*, first published in 1845, in which she says: 'The rhubarb for these should be of good sort, quickly grown, and tender . . . The young stalks look well when left the length of the dish in which they are served, and only slightly encrusted with the batter through which they should be merely drawn.'

The fritters must be eaten very hot.

SERVES 6

For the batter

scant 150ml/¼ pint boiling water
50g/2oz butter, cut into pieces
scant 450ml/¾ pint cold water
350g/12oz plain white flour
2 large egg whites

For the fruit

900g/2lb rhubarb, trimmed
sunflower oil
100g/4oz caster sugar

Cut the rhubarb into 15cm/6in lengths and then cut each piece lengthways into strips about the size of a little finger.

Pour the boiling water onto the butter in a bowl and stir until the butter has melted. Add the cold water, then gradually mix the liquid into the flour, stirring well to make a smooth batter. Whisk the egg whites until stiff but not dry, then fold into the batter with a metal spoon.

Pour about 25mm/1in of oil into a large frying pan and heat until very hot. Draw the rhubarb pieces through the batter, then let the batter drip off again until the rhubarb is just visible. Fry 3 or 4 pieces at a time, for a few minutes, until the rhubarb is tender and the fritters are a pale golden brown. Drain the pieces of rhubarb on absorbent kitchen paper, then pile onto a warm plate and sprinkle with sugar. Serve immediately, with cream.

VARIATION

This batter can also be used for round slices of peeled and cored apple, peeled orange or skinned (see page 162), halved and stoned apricots or peaches.

Spiced Apple Pancake

We were surprised to find this dish in Elinor Fettiplace's *Receipt Book* (1604) because it is similar to the Austrian Kaiserschmarren (see page 128). Our version is like a light soufflé and must be eaten as soon as it is cooked.

SERVES 2
use a frying pan about 24cm/9½in in diameter

225g/8oz Bramley cooking apples, peeled, cored and thinly sliced
1 tbsp cold water
2 egg whites
25g/1oz caster sugar, plus a little extra for sprinkling
15g/½oz plain white flour
pinch of ground cloves
¼ tsp ground cinnamon
4 tbsp double cream
15g/½oz unsalted butter

Put the apples with the water into a saucepan and cook over a low heat, stirring continuously, until the apples are soft, then beat until smooth. Leave the purée to cool completely.

Preheat the grill to maximum.

Whisk the egg whites until stiff but not dry. Mix together the sugar, flour and spices and fold them into the egg whites with a metal spoon. Gently fold the cream and apple purée into the mixture.

Melt the butter in a heavy frying pan and heat until very hot, but not brown. Pour in the apple mixture, shake the pan to level the surface and lower the temperature after a few moments. Cook the pancake for 2–3 minutes, then loosen the sides with a spatula and place under the grill until the pancake is golden brown.

Serve immediately from the pan, breaking the pancake into large pieces and sprinkling with a little caster sugar.

CHAPTER 7

ICE CREAMS AND SORBETS

Blackberry Ice Cream
Brown Bread Ice Cream with Rum
Lemon Curd Ice Cream
Chestnut Ice Cream with Brandy
Ginger, Whisky and Honey Ice Cream
Orange Ice Cream
Pear and Ratafia Ice Cream
Raspberry and Redcurrant Ice Cream
Rose Petal Ice Cream
Shakespeare's Iced Pudding
Vanilla Ice Cream
Rhubarb Sorbet
Apricot Sorbet
Pear Sorbet
Spiced Cider Sorbet
Tea Sorbet with Rum
Elderflower Sorbet

According to Jane Grigson in Good Things *(1971), the first British ice house, where large blocks of ice were stored to keep food cold throughout the year, was built by Charles II in 1660. Apparently, the first ice cream in Britain was eaten at Windsor Castle in 1677. Soon, nearly all the great houses followed suit by building their own ice houses and serving ice creams and sorbets as a delicacy, using fresh fruit from their orchards and kitchen gardens.*

At one stage, ice creams and sorbets went out of fashion as a serious pudding but this is not the case today. With our domestic freezers, electric food processors and easily available fresh ingredients, making ice cream at home has become very simple. Home-made ice creams and sorbets are a real treat and have now rightly regained their former stature.

Blackberry Ice Cream

A simple, but delectable ice cream. Our hedgerows are prolific with wild blackberries in early autumn and we always look forward to picking them, especially as they tend to have so much more flavour than the cultivated ones. The fruit has not been sieved, which we feel gives it a more interesting texture.

SERVES 6
use a 1.5 litre/2½ pint plastic freezerproof container

450g/1lb blackberries
100g/4oz caster sugar
300ml/½ pint double cream, lightly whipped

Put the blackberries and sugar into a heavy-based saucepan and heat gently until the sugar has dissolved and the juice has started to run. Purée the fruit, leave to cool, then fold in the cream.

Put the ice cream into the plastic freezerproof container and freeze for several hours until mushy. Process the half frozen mixture thoroughly in a food processor, or beat well in an electric mixer, then return to the freezer until it is completely frozen.

Take the ice cream out of the freezer about 1 hour before serving and leave it in the fridge.

Serve with Almond, Hazelnut or Walnut Biscuits (see page 175).

BROWN BREAD ICE CREAM WITH RUM

A really special old-fashioned ice cream, generously laced with rum. Caramelising the breadcrumbs makes them deliciously crunchy and quite unrecognisable.

SERVES 6
use a 1.5 litre/2½ pint plastic freezerproof container

sunflower oil for greasing
100g/4oz brown breadcrumbs
100g/4oz light muscovado sugar
300ml/½ pint double cream
300ml/½ pint single cream
2 tbsp rum
1 large egg white

Preheat the oven to 200°C/400°F/Gas Mark 6.

Brush a baking sheet with oil. Mix the breadcrumbs and sugar together and spread on the baking sheet. Bake for about 15 minutes until the sugar caramelises, then allow to cool and break the crumbs up again.

Whip the creams together until they form soft peaks, stir in the caramelised breadcrumbs and rum, then put the mixture into the freezerproof plastic container and freeze for several hours until mushy.

Whisk the egg white until stiff, but not dry. Beat the half frozen ice cream by hand or lightly in an electric mixer, then fold in the egg white with a metal spoon. Put the ice cream back into the freezer until it is completely frozen.

Take the ice cream out of the freezer about 1 hour before serving and leave it in the fridge.

Serve with a hot or cold fruit sauce.

Lemon Curd Ice Cream

If you have a weakness for lemon curd you will love this ice cream. It can be decorated with some extra lemon rind, cut into very fine strips and simmered in a little water for 2–3 minutes, then drained, rinsed in cold water and dried.

SERVES 6
use a 1.5 litre/2½ pint plastic freezerproof container

3 medium eggs, lightly beaten
225g/8oz caster sugar
100g/4oz butter, cut into small pieces
finely grated rind of 3 large lemons
175ml/6fl oz lemon juice
150ml/¼ pint single cream
150ml/¼ pint double cream, lightly whipped
1 large egg white

Put the eggs, sugar, butter, lemon rind and juice into the top of a double boiler or a bowl set over a pan of simmering water. Stir the mixture continuously until it is thick. Pour the curd into a bowl, leave to cool completely, then stir in the single cream and fold in the double cream. Put the mixture into a plastic freezerproof container and freeze for several hours until mushy.

Whisk the egg white until stiff, but not dry. Process the half frozen mixture thoroughly in a food processor, or beat well in an electric mixer. Fold in the egg white with a metal spoon, then put the ice cream back into the freezer until it is completely frozen.

Take the ice cream out of the freezer about 1 hour before serving and leave it in the fridge.

Serve with Almond, Hazelnut or Walnut Biscuits (see page 175).

Chestnut Ice Cream with Brandy

This is a rich autumnal ice cream.

Chestnuts are easily peeled using a microwave oven. Cut a cross in the flat part of the outer skin with a pointed knife, then place about 6 chestnuts well apart on a plate and microwave on high power for 1–2 minutes. Shake the plate halfway through the cooking time, then remove the chestnuts and peel off the outer and inner skin. If they do not peel easily, microwave them for a little longer. Alternatively, make a cut in the flat part of the outer skin of the chestnuts and put a few at a time into boiling water for 2 minutes, then peel as above.

SERVES 6

use a 1.5 litre/2½ pint plastic freezerproof container

450g/1lb chestnuts, peeled (see above)
300ml/½ pint cold milk
150ml/¼ pint cold water
3 tbsp lemon juice
175g/6oz light muscovado sugar
4 tbsp brandy
150ml/¼ pint double cream
150ml/¼ pint single cream
1 large egg white

Put the chestnuts into a saucepan with the milk and water, then cover and simmer them for about 30 minutes or until the chestnuts are tender. Purée the mixture in a food processor or blender, or rub through a fine sieve. Add the lemon juice gradually to the purée until it is completely smooth, then mix in the sugar. Leave the mixture to cool and stir in the brandy. Lightly whip the creams together, then fold into the chestnut mixture. Put the mixture into a plastic freezerproof container. Freeze the ice cream for several hours until mushy.

Whisk the egg white until stiff, but not dry. Process the half frozen ice cream thoroughly in a food processor or beat well in an electric mixer, then fold in the egg white with a metal spoon.

Put the ice cream back into the freezer until it is completely frozen.

Take the ice cream out of the freezer about 1 hour before serving and keep it at room temperature.

Serve with bitter chocolate biscuits.

Ginger, Whisky and Honey Ice Cream

A luxurious tasting, very gingery ice cream.

SERVES 6

use a 1.5 litre/2½ pint plastic freezerproof container

300ml/½ pint cold milk
150g/5oz preserved ginger
175g/6oz honey
3 tbsp lemon juice
5–7 tbsp whisky
600ml/1 pint double cream, lightly whipped

Purée 75g/3oz of the ginger with the milk in a food processor or blender until they are smooth. Mix in the honey, lemon juice and whisky. Fold in the cream. Put the mixture into a plastic freezerproof container and freeze for several hours until mushy.

Process the half frozen mixture thoroughly in a food processor, or beat well in an electric mixer. Chop the remaining ginger into small pieces and stir into the ice cream mixture. Put the ice cream back into the freezer until it is completely frozen.

Serve straight from the freezer with Macaroons or Shortbread (see pages 176 and 177).

ORANGE ICE CREAM

We tried a recipe for Orange Fool from *The Art of Cookery* by Hannah Glasse, first published in 1760 and decided that we preferred it frozen as an ice cream.

Some Chocolate Orange Rind is delicious served with the ice cream: cut the rind off 2 large oranges and remove the pith. Cut the rind into thin strips and blanch them in simmering water for 2 minutes, then drain and refresh in cold water. Dry the strips well with absorbent kitchen paper. Melt about 100g/4oz of bitter chocolate and dip about half of each strip of rind into it. Leave the coated pieces of rind on a sheet of greaseproof paper to dry, then chill in the fridge and serve on the same day.

SERVES 8
use a 2 litre/3½ pint plastic freezerproof container

750ml/1¼ pints orange juice
600ml/1 pint double cream
6 medium eggs, lightly beaten
100g/4oz caster sugar
¼ tsp ground cinnamon
freshly grated nutmeg
15g/½oz butter

Put the orange juice and cream in a saucepan and heat to just below boiling point. Put the rest of the ingredients together with the warm orange juice and cream into the top of a double boiler or in a basin set over a saucepan of simmering water. Stir the mixture until it thickens, then pour into a bowl and leave to cool.

Put the mixture into the plastic freezerproof container and freeze for several hours until mushy. Process the half frozen ice cream thoroughly in a food processor, or beat well in an electric mixer, then return to the freezer until it is completely frozen.

Take the ice cream out of the freezer about 1 hour before serving and keep it at room temperature.

Serve scattered with Chocolate Orange Rind (see above) and Almond, Hazelnut or Walnut Biscuits (see pages 176 and 177).

Pear and Ratafia Ice Cream

The idea for an ice cream with pears came from Hilary Spurling's version of Elinor Fettiplace's *Receipt Book of Elizabethan Country House Cooking* (1604): 'Wardens may be chopped and mixed with whipped cream to make a memorable ice.'

Sprinkle lemon juice straight onto the pears as soon as they are cut to stop them turning brown.

SERVES 6
use a 1.5 litre/2½ pint plastic freezerproof container

300ml/½ pint double cream
150ml/¼ pint single cream
2 large ripe pears, peeled, cored and cut into pieces
3 tbsp runny honey
2 tbsp lemon juice
4 tbsp rosewater (see page 179)
50g/2oz ratafia biscuits (see page 179), roughly chopped
1 large egg white

Lightly whip the creams together, then stir in the pear pieces with the honey, lemon juice, rosewater and the ratafia biscuits. Put the mixture into the freezerproof container and freeze for several hours until mushy.

Whisk the egg white until stiff, but not dry. Beat the half frozen ice cream by hand or lightly in an electric mixer and fold in the egg white with a metal spoon. Put the ice cream back into the freezer until it is completely frozen.

Take the ice cream out of the freezer about 1 hour before serving and put it in the fridge.

Serve with chocolate leaves and Almond, Hazelnut or Walnut Biscuits (see pages 176 and 177).

Raspberry and Redcurrant Ice Cream

This raspberry ice cream has whole redcurrants in it. The redcurrants stay frozen and quite crisp, rather like pearls of water ice scattered through the ice cream.

SERVES 6
use a 1.5 litre/2½ pint plastic freezerproof container

450g/1lb raspberries
175g/6oz caster sugar
300ml/½ pint single cream
150ml/¼ pint double cream
175g/6oz redcurrants, stripped from their stalk

Purée the raspberries in a food processor or blender, then mix in the sugar. Lightly whip the creams together and fold into the purée.

Put the mixture in a plastic freezerproof container and freeze for several hours until mushy.

Process the half frozen mixture thoroughly in a food processor, or beat well in an electric mixer. Fold in the redcurrants by hand, making sure that they are evenly distributed. Put the ice cream back into the freezer until it is completely frozen.

Take the ice cream out of the freezer about 1 hour before serving and leave it in the fridge.

Serve with Macaroons or Shortbread (see pages 176 and 177).

Rose Petal Ice Cream

The idea for this pretty ice cream came from Hilary Spurling's version of Elinor Fettiplace's *Receipt Book of Elizabethan Country House Cooking* (1604). Pick the roses first thing in the morning, but beware of choosing those which have been sprayed with insecticide. They should be neither in bud nor fully blown. Cut off the yellow tips at the base of the petals.

SERVES 6
use a 1.5 litre/2½ pint plastic freezerproof container

50g/2oz fragrant damask rose petals
120ml/4fl oz cold water
350g/12oz caster sugar
3 tbsp lemon juice
1 tbsp rosewater (see page 179)
600ml/1 pint double cream, lightly whipped
2 large egg whites

Simmer the rose petals in the water, covered, for about 10 minutes until they are tender and have lost their colour, then gradually add the sugar, stirring, until it has dissolved. Bring to the boil, then remove from the heat and leave to cool a little, before adding the lemon juice and rosewater.

Put the mixture into a food processor and process briefly, in short bursts, to break the petals into small pieces, then leave to cool completely.

Fold in the cream, then put the mixture into the plastic freezerproof container and freeze for several hours until mushy.

Whisk the egg whites until stiff, but not dry. Process the half frozen ice cream in a food processor, or beat it in an electric mixer, then fold in the egg whites with a metal spoon. Put the ice cream back in the freezer until it is completely frozen.

Take the ice cream out of the freezer about 1 hour before serving and put it in the fridge.

Serve with Almond, Hazelnut or Walnut Biscuits (see pages 176 and 177).

Shakespeare's Iced Pudding

This is one of several personalised iced puddings in *The Royal English and Foreign Confectioner* by Charles Elme Francatelli, published in 1862. Others include Iced Pudding à la Victoria, à la Shelley and à la Kemble.

A luxurious ice cream, this pudding is packed with dried fruit and pistachio nuts. Don't be surprised by the dramatic colour change when the Blue Curaçao is added which turns the ice cream a soft pale green.

SERVES 6
use a 1.5 litre/2½ pint plastic freezerproof container

For the custard

300ml/½ pint double cream
4 medium egg yolks
25g/1oz caster sugar

For the caramel

50g/2oz caster sugar
5cm/2in cinnamon stick
finely pared rind of ½ lemon
150ml/¼ pint boiling water
4 tbsp Blue Curaçao

For the fruit, nuts and cream

25g/1oz candied orange peel, finely chopped
25g/1oz shelled pistachio nuts, chopped
25g/1oz dried pears, finely chopped
25g/1oz dried pineapple, finely chopped
250ml/8fl oz double cream, lightly whipped

Make a custard with the cream, egg yolks and sugar (see page 173), then leave to cool, stirring now and then.

Put the sugar, cinnamon stick and lemon rind into a heavy-based saucepan and heat gently until the sugar has dissolved, then simmer until it caramelises and turns golden brown. Mix in the water and stir the caramel until smooth. Leave it to cool a little, then take out the cinnamon stick and lemon rind. Stir the caramel into the custard together with the Blue Curaçao. Put the mixture into the plastic freezerproof container and freeze for several hours until mushy.

Process the half frozen mixture thoroughly in a food processor or beat well in an electric mixer. Stir in the fruit and nuts and fold in the cream. Put the ice cream back into the freezer until it is completely frozen.

Take the ice cream out of the freezer about 45 minutes before serving and leave it in the fridge.

Serve with Macaroons or Shortbread (see pages 176 and 177).

Vanilla Ice Cream

This is probably the most popular of ice creams. However, many versions are a travesty of the real thing. It is essential to use a very fresh vanilla pod. Vanilla Ice Cream goes very well with almost any pudding.

SERVES 4–6
use a 1 litre/1¾ pint plastic freezerproof container

2 medium eggs
2 medium egg yolks
100g/4oz caster sugar
300ml/½ pint single cream
vanilla pod
300ml/½ pint double cream, lightly whipped

Beat the eggs, egg yolks and sugar together. Put the single cream into a small, heavy-based saucepan, then split the vanilla pod in half lengthways and scrape the seeds into the cream. Add the pod to the cream and heat to just below boiling point. Mix the cream with the vanilla pod into the eggs and sugar and put the mixture into the top of a double boiler or in a basin set over a saucepan of simmering water. Stir the custard mixture for about

10 minutes until it has thickened (see page 173). Leave it to cool, then take out the vanilla pod and fold in the double cream.

Put the ice cream into the plastic freezerproof container and freeze for several hours until mushy. Process the half frozen mixture thoroughly in a food processor, or beat well in an electric mixer, then put it back in the freezer until it is completely frozen.

Take the ice cream out of the freezer about 15 minutes before serving and put it in the fridge.

Serve with Almond, Hazelnut or Walnut Biscuits (see page 175), with other ice creams, sorbets, fruit or puddings.

Rhubarb Sorbet

A beautiful, marshmallow-pink sorbet with a delicate, fresh flavour.

SERVES 6

use a 1 litre/1¾ pint plastic freezerproof container

900g/2lb pink rhubarb, trimmed and cut into 25mm/1in pieces
225g/8oz caster sugar
7 tbsp orange juice
1 large egg white

Preheat the oven to 170°C/325°F/Gas Mark 3.

Put the rhubarb and sugar into an ovenproof dish and cook, covered, for about 1 hour, until the rhubarb is very tender and has produced a lot of juice. Strain the rhubarb well, discard the fruit and leave the juice to cool.

Add the orange juice to the rhubarb juice, then transfer to the plastic freezerproof container and freeze for several hours until mushy.

Whisk the egg white until stiff, but not dry. Process the half frozen mixture thoroughly in a food processor, or beat well in an electric mixer, then fold in the egg white with a metal spoon. Put it back into the freezer until it is completely frozen. Serve straight from the freezer, with cream and Almond, Hazelnut or Walnut Biscuits (see page 175).

Apricot Sorbet

This is a lovely, fresh, golden-orange sorbet with a strong apricot flavour.

SERVES 4–6
use a 1.5 litre/2½ pint plastic freezerproof container

450g/1lb apricots
150g/5oz caster sugar
300ml/½ pint cold water
3 tbsp lemon juice
2 medium egg whites

Steam the whole apricots, covered, in a vegetable steamer or metal colander over simmering water until they are just tender, then take out the stones and purée the fruit.

Put the sugar and water in a saucepan and bring slowly to simmering point. When the sugar has dissolved, boil the syrup for 5 minutes. Stir the syrup and lemon juice into the apricot purée. Leave the purée to cool, then freeze for several hours until mushy.

Whisk the egg whites until stiff, but not dry. Process the half frozen mixture thoroughly in a food processor, or beat well in an electric mixer, then fold in the egg white with a metal spoon and put the sorbet back in the freezer until it is completely frozen.

Serve straight from the freezer, with cream and Almond, Hazelnut or Walnut Biscuits (see page 175).

Pear Sorbet

This sorbet has a very intense pear flavour and the pears used for it must be properly ripe, but *not* overripe. It is therefore probably best to buy some pears that are a little underripe and keep them on a windowsill until they seem just right. Sprinkle lemon juice onto the pears as soon as they are cut to stop them turning brown.

SERVES 6
use a 1.5 litre/2½ pint plastic freezerproof container

300ml/½ pint cold water
175g/6oz caster sugar
900g/2lb ripe pears, peeled, cored and quartered
3 tbsp lemon juice • 2 egg whites

Put the water and sugar into a saucepan and heat gently until the sugar has dissolved. Bring to the boil and boil for 5 minutes. Leave the syrup to cool a little. Purée the pears with the lemon juice and add the syrup. Put the mixture into the plastic freezerproof container and freeze for several hours until mushy.

Whisk the egg whites until stiff, but not dry. Process the half frozen mixture thoroughly in a food processor or beat well with an electric mixer, then fold in the egg white with a metal spoon. Put the sorbet back into the freezer until it is completely frozen.

Take the sorbet out of the freezer about 15 minutes before serving and put it in the fridge. Serve with Macaroons or Shortbread (see pages 176 and 177).

Spiced Cider Sorbet

A light apple-based sorbet. This is good served with a variety of different flavoured ice creams as well as on its own.

SERVES 6–8
use a 1.5 litre/2½ pint plastic freezerproof container

400ml/¾ pint pressed apple juice
5 whole cloves
10cm/4in cinnamon stick
4 tbsp honey
600ml/1 pint sweet cider
1 large egg white

Put the apple juice with the cloves and cinnamon stick into a saucepan and bring to the boil. Add the honey, cover the saucepan and leave until cold to infuse.

Take out the cloves and cinnamon stick, stir in the cider, then transfer the liquid to the plastic freezerproof container and freeze for several hours until mushy.

Whisk the egg white until stiff, but not dry. Process the half frozen mixture thoroughly in a food processor, or beat it well in an electric mixer, then fold in the egg white with a metal spoon. Put the sorbet back into the freezer until it is completely frozen.

Serve straight from the freezer, with cream and bitter chocolate biscuits.

Tea Sorbet with Rum

The flavour of this sorbet is similar to iced tea and is very refreshing on a hot summer's day, served with fresh chopped mint leaves.

SERVES 6

use a 1.5 litre/2½ pint plastic freezerproof container

600ml/1 pint water, freshly boiled
15g/½oz Darjeeling tea leaves
100g/4oz caster sugar
2 tbsp rum
1 tbsp lemon juice
1 large egg white

Warm a jug, then add the boiling water and tea leaves and leave to infuse for 5 minutes. Strain the tea through a fine sieve and stir in the sugar until it has completely dissolved. Mix in the rum and lemon juice. Leave the mixture until completely cold, then put in the plastic freezerproof container and freeze for several hours until mushy.

Whisk the egg white until stiff, but not dry. Process the half frozen mixture thoroughly in a food processor, or beat well in an electric mixer. Fold in the egg white with a metal spoon. Put the sorbet back into the freezer until it is completely frozen.

Serve straight from the freezer, with Macaroons or Shortbread (see pages 176 and 177).

Elderflower Sorbet

Elderflowers have a very distinctive, almost muscat-like taste and make a delightfully refreshing, unusual sorbet. If fresh elderflowers are not easily available, put 4 tbsp elderflower cordial (which is sold at good supermarkets and wholefood shops) into the cold syrup instead. This sorbet is especially good served with a selection of different ice creams or fruit.

SERVES 6

use a 1.5 litre/2½ pint plastic freezerproof container

100g/4oz caster sugar
600ml/1 pint cold water
1 handful of fresh young elderflowers, thick stems removed
3 tbsp lemon juice
1 large egg white

Put the sugar and water into a saucepan and heat gently until the sugar has dissolved. Bring to the boil and boil for 5 minutes. Take the pan off the heat, immerse the flowerheads in the syrup and leave them until the syrup is completely cold. Strain the syrup through a piece of muslin, stir in the lemon juice, then put the syrup into the plastic freezerproof container and freeze for several hours until mushy.

Whisk the egg white until stiff, but not dry. Process the half frozen mixture thoroughly in a food processor, or beat it well in an electric mixer. Fold in the egg white with a metal spoon and put the sorbet back into the freezer until it is completely frozen. Serve straight from the freezer, with Macaroons or Shortbread (see pages 176 and 177).

CHAPTER 8

ORCHARD, FIELD AND HEDGEROW

Apple Snow
Bramleys Baked with Honey
Hot Chestnuts and Prunes with Orange
Christmas Plum Mincemeat
Mulled Peaches and Apricots with Redcurrants
Pears Poached in Ginger Wine
Poached Vanilla Cherries with Fresh Mint
Raspberry, Cherry and Redcurrant Sago Pudding
Strawberries Marinated in Honey and Rum
Strawberry Shortcakes with Raspberry Sauce
Summer Pudding
See also Blackberry and Elderflower recipes

The temperate British climate is most conducive to growing fruit, which is one of the main ingredients of many British puddings. British apples are among the best in the world and give us a tremendous start, hence our enormous range of apple dishes. We not only produce an excellent range of eating apples; we also grow a unique cooking apple, the Bramley, which is crisp, juicy, full of flavour and ideal for baking whole, making into purées or slicing into pies.

Our currants and berries, too, are used extensively, both raw and cooked, and are some of the best in the world. Summer Pudding is a celebration of British soft fruit and is unsurpassed.

Apple Snow

'A pretty Supper Dish' according to Mrs Beeton. Apple purée is a very soothing pudding, with or without the egg whites.

SERVES 6

use a 2.1 litre/3½ pint glass or china dish, 6 glasses or 6 large ramekins 80mm/3¼in in diameter and 45mm/1¾in high

900g/2lb cooking apples, peeled, cored and thinly sliced
thinly pared rind of ½ lemon
100g/4oz caster sugar
4 medium egg whites

Put the apple, lemon rind and sugar into a heavy-based saucepan and cook over a very low heat, stirring now and then, until the apple is tender. Take out the lemon rind, purée the apple and leave to cool.

Whisk the egg whites until stiff, but not dry, and fold into the apple purée with a metal spoon. Put the snow into the dish, glasses or ramekins and chill.

Serve chilled, with cream, Custard Sauce (see page 173), Vanilla Ice Cream (see page 148) or natural yogurt and Macaroons or Shortbread (see pages 176 and 177).

VARIATION

A cinnamon stick, a little ground cinnamon or 2–3 whole cloves can be cooked with the apples to flavour them.

Bramleys Baked with Honey

Choose an ovenproof dish in which the apples will fit tightly. They need to be roughly the same size. When they are baked, the Bramleys rise and become fluffy with a buttery, syrup sauce.

SERVES 4
use a shallow ovenproof dish (see above)

25g/1oz butter, plus a little extra for greasing
4 Bramley apples, each weighing about 175g/6oz
1 tbsp cold water
ground cinnamon
4 tbsp honey

Preheat the oven to 180°C/350°F/Gas Mark 4.

Generously butter the dish. Core the apples and score the skin around the middle of each apple with the point of a knife. Arrange the apples in the dish and add the water. Put a small piece of the butter into each apple, followed by a pinch of cinnamon and a tablespoonful of honey. Put the rest of the butter on top of the apples and bake for 30–35 minutes until tender, basting from time to time with the buttery juices.

Serve with cream, Custard Sauce (see page 173), Vanilla Ice Cream (see page 148) or natural yogurt.

Hot Chestnuts and Prunes with Orange

This recipe has been adapted from one in *The Gentle Art of Cookery* by Mrs C. F. Leyel and Miss Olga Hartley, first published in 1925. It is a delicious, subtle mixture of winter fruit.

SERVES 4
use a 1.5 litre/2½ pint dish

450g/1lb no-need-to soak prunes, stoned
10cm/4in cinnamon stick
350g/12oz chestnuts
1 large orange, peeled, pith removed, sliced thinly and cut into pieces
50g/2oz light muscovado sugar
2 tbsp lemon juice
75ml/3fl oz sherry

Put the prunes into a saucepan with the cinnamon stick and enough water to just cover them. Simmer gently until just tender. Take out the cinnamon stick, drain the prunes, reserving the juice.

Preheat the oven to 230°C/450°F/Gas Mark 8.

Meanwhile, roast the chestnuts. Make a cross in the flat part of the skin with the point of a sharp knife and place on a baking tray. Roast for 10–15 minutes. Take off the skins and chop the chestnuts fairly finely.

Mix the prunes and chestnuts together in a dish with the pieces of orange. Measure 150ml/¼ pint of the reserved hot prune juice and stir in the sugar until it has dissolved. Add the lemon juice and sherry and pour the juice over the chestnuts and fruit.

Serve immediately, with cream, Vanilla Ice Cream (see page 148) or natural yogurt and Macaroons or Shortbread (see pages 176 and 177).

Christmas Plum Mincemeat

This is a very light, spicy mincemeat, loaded with fruit, nuts and brandy and made without fat. It is based on a recipe from *Farmhouse Fare, Country Recipes collected by the Farmers Weekly*, first published in 1935. It is perfect for Mincemeat Plate Pie (see page 19) or for Star Mince Pies (see page 22) and will keep for several days in the fridge or several weeks in the freezer.

The cooked plums should yield about 300ml/½ pint of purée.

MAKES ABOUT 1.75KG/4LB

450g/1lb plums, cut into pieces
1 tbsp lemon juice
100g/4oz currants
100g/4oz raisins
100g/4oz sultanas
50g/2oz candied orange rind, finely chopped
50g/2oz candied lemon rind, finely chopped
100g/4oz blanched almonds, finely chopped
finely grated rind of 1 lemon
6g/¼oz ground ginger
6g/¼oz ground cinnamon
6g/¼oz ground cloves
675g/1½lb cooking apples, peeled, cored and finely chopped
175g/6oz dark muscovado sugar
5 tbsp brandy

Preheat the oven to 170°C/325°F/Gas Mark 3.

Put the plums and lemon juice into a heavy casserole, cover with a lid and cook for 20–30 minutes until the plums are tender. Press the plums through a fairly coarse sieve. Leave the purée to cool.

Meanwhile, mix together the currants, raisins, sultanas, candied rind, almonds and grated lemon rind. Stir in the plum purée, cover the fruit and leave the mixture in the fridge overnight.

Add the spices, apples, sugar and brandy, stirring it all together well. Use the mincemeat at once or store as above.

Mulled Peaches and Apricots with Redcurrants

To skin the peaches, put them in boiling water for 1–2 minutes, then pierce the skin with the point of a knife and peel it off. Peaches and apricots that are just ripe, but not overripe are best for this recipe.

SERVES 4–6
use a 2.4 litre/4 pint glass or china dish

300ml/½ pint sweet white wine
150ml/¼ pint cold water
100g/4oz caster sugar
3 whole cloves
10cm/4in cinnamon stick, broken in half
small blade of mace
1 bay leaf
3 strips of orange rind
2 strips of lemon rind
4 large ripe peaches, skinned (see above), stoned and quartered
450g/1lb ripe apricots, stoned and halved
175g/6oz redcurrants, stripped from the stalk

Put the wine, water, sugar, cloves, cinnamon stick, mace, bay leaf and orange and lemon rind into a large heavy-based saucepan and heat gently until the sugar has dissolved, then bring to the boil. Boil the syrup for 3 minutes.

Simmer the peaches and apricots in the syrup for 5 minutes. Bring the fruit back to the boil, stir in the redcurrants, then turn off the heat and leave the fruit to cool. Take out the cloves, cinnamon stick, mace, rind and bay leaf.

Serve warm or cold, with cream, Custard Sauce (see page 173), Vanilla Ice Cream (see page 148) or natural yogurt and Macaroons or Shortbread (see pages 176 and 177).

Pears Poached in Ginger Wine

A delicious alternative to Pears in Red Wine. Sprinkle the pears with 25g/1oz toasted flaked almonds (see page 180) or some chocolate leaves or curls if they are being served cold.

Immerse the pears immediately after peeling them in a bowl of water with some lemon juice in it to prevent them from turning brown.

SERVES 6
use a 2.4 litre/4 pint glass or china dish

600ml/1 pint ginger wine
100g/4oz caster sugar
6 medium Conference pears, peeled whole with stalks intact
10cm/4in cinnamon stick
2 whole cloves
2 tbsp lemon juice, plus a little extra

Preheat the oven to 180°C/350°F/Gas Mark 4.

Put the ginger wine and sugar into a saucepan, heat gently until the sugar has dissolved, then bring to the boil.

Arrange the pears in an ovenproof dish with the cinnamon stick and cloves, then pour over the ginger syrup and cover the dish with a lid. Cook the pears in the oven for about 45 minutes, or until they are just tender, turning them halfway through the cooking time.

Put the pears into the glass or china dish and reduce the ginger syrup to about 300ml/½ pint by fast boiling without a lid, then take out the cinnamon stick and cloves, stir in the lemon juice, leave the syrup to cool and pour over the fruit.

Serve warm or cold (see above), with cream or Vanilla Ice Cream (see page 148).

Poached Vanilla Cherries with Fresh Mint

The contrast of colours and flavours in this dish are a delight, but the mint takes over if it is left on the cherries for too long.

SERVES 4
use a 1.2 litre/2 pint glass or china dish

300ml/½ pint cold water
50g/2oz caster sugar
vanilla pod
675g/1½lb cherries, stalks removed
about 2 tbsp chopped mint leaves

Put the water, sugar and vanilla pod into a saucepan, heat gently until the sugar has dissolved, then boil for 3 minutes.

Simmer the cherries in the syrup for 5 minutes, then leave to cool and take out the vanilla pod. Transfer to the glass or china dish and scatter the mint over the cherries *just before* serving.

Serve warm or cold, with cream, Vanilla Ice Cream (see page 148) or natural yogurt and Macaroons or Shortbread (see pages 176 and 177).

Raspberry, Cherry and Redcurrant Sago Pudding

Sago is an edible starch taken from the pith of a species of palm tree that grows in the East Indies and the islands of the Indian Ocean. It is often associated with milk puddings, but when it is cooked it turns from white to transparent and is jelly-like in texture. Here we have used it to lightly set the fruit. The purée is not sieved so that some pips will remain. It is like a thick compote with an intense taste of summer fruit.

SERVES 6
use a 900ml/1½ pint glass or china dish

400g/14oz raspberries
350g/12oz redcurrants, stripped from the stalk
225g/8oz cherries, stalks removed and stoned
600ml/1 pint cold water
225g/8oz caster sugar
50g/2oz sago

Put the raspberries, redcurrants and cherries into a saucepan with the water. Bring to simmering point and simmer for about 5 minutes until the juices start to run.

Purée the fruit, stir in the sugar and sago, then bring the mixture back to the boil and simmer for 20 minutes, stirring frequently. Pour the pudding into the dish. Leave to cool, then chill.

Serve chilled, with cream, Vanilla Ice Cream (see page 148), natural yogurt or Mrs Beeton's Quaking Pudding (see page 107).

Strawberries Marinated in Honey and Rum

A useful dish for entertaining as it must be prepared well in advance. It is important that the strawberries are neither under nor overripe.

SERVES 2–3
use a 900ml/1½ pint glass or china dish

350g/12oz strawberries, hulled
2 tbsp honey
2 tbsp orange juice
3 tbsp rum

Thickly slice the strawberries and put them into the dish. Mix together the honey, orange juice and rum, then pour over the strawberries. Leave in the fridge to marinate for 24 hours.

Serve lightly chilled with cream, Vanilla Ice Cream (see page 148) or natural yogurt and Almond, Hazelnut or Walnut Biscuits (see page 175).

Strawberry Shortcakes with Raspberry Sauce

Strawberry Shortcakes are essentially British and are now often made with a double layer of crisp shortbread biscuit. In this recipe, the shortcake is thicker and more like a sponge cake with the strawberries and cream piled on top.

MAKES 14
use 2 baking sheets

For the shortcake

250g/9oz plain white flour
1 tsp baking powder
175g/6oz butter, chilled, and cut into pieces, plus a little extra for greasing
150g/30z caster sugar
1 medium egg

For the cream and fruit

2 tbsp vanilla sugar (see page 179)
600ml/1 pint double cream, lightly whipped
900g/2lb strawberries, hulled
mint leaves, to decorate

For the sauce

675g/1½lb raspberries
175g/6oz caster sugar
75ml/3fl oz orange juice

Preheat the oven to 230°C/450°F/Gas Mark 8 and lightly butter the baking sheets.

To make the shortcake, put the flour, baking powder, butter and sugar into a food processor and process until they resemble breadcrumbs, then add the egg and process the mixture briefly to form a smooth dough. Alternatively, mix the baking powder into the flour and rub in the butter by hand until it resembles breadcrumbs, then stir in the sugar, add the egg and knead the mixture until it forms a smooth dough.

Roll out the dough on a lightly floured surface to about 6mm/¼in thick and cut out 14 circles with a 75mm/3in pastry cutter. Arrange the shortcakes fairly well spaced out on the baking sheets and bake for about 10 minutes until pale golden. Put the shortcakes on a wire rack and leave to cool completely.

To make the Raspberry Sauce see page 113.

Fold the vanilla sugar into the cream and spoon some over each shortcake. Pile the strawberries on top.

Serve immediately decorated with mint leaves and with Raspberry Sauce.

SUMMER PUDDING

The simplest of ideas that makes an unbeatable, quintessentially British pudding. Make it at least 24 hours before you need it so that the fruit juices can soak right through the bread, which should be at least a day old. The proportions of summer berries can be varied according to taste and availability.

SERVES 6–8
use a 1.5 litre/2½ pint pudding basin

550g/1¼lb raspberries
225g/8oz redcurrants, stripped from the stalk
100g/4oz blackcurrants, stripped from the stalk
175g/6oz caster sugar
about 9 slices white bread, crusts removed

Put the fruit and sugar into a heavy-based saucepan and cook over a low heat. Shake the pan from time to time, until the sugar has dissolved and the fruit juices have started to run, stirring gently once.

Meanwhile, line the pudding basin with the bread, pressing the edges together to make a good seal. Fill the basin with the warm fruit (reserving 2–3 tbsp of the juice), then cover it with a layer of bread. Seal the rim well. Put a saucer on top of the pudding with a heavy weight on it. Leave in the fridge for at least 24 hours.

Loosen the edges of the pudding with a knife and turn out onto a deep plate. Pour the reserved juice over the pudding in any places where the fruit juices have not soaked through.

Serve lightly chilled, with cream or Vanilla Ice Cream (see page 148).

ACCOMPANIMENTS

Brandy or Rum Butter
Brandy Sauce
Custard Sauce
Port Wine Sauce
Almond, Hazelnut or Walnut Biscuits
Macaroons
Shortbread

Brandy or Rum Butter

This is sometimes served with Mince Pies (see page 22) or with Christmas Pudding (see pages 75 and 76) together with Brandy Sauce (see page 172) or cream.

SERVES ABOUT 8

100g/4oz unsalted butter, softened
100g/4oz caster sugar
4 tbsp brandy

Beat the butter and sugar together until very pale and fluffy, then gradually add the brandy, beating the mixture all the time. Transfer to a dish and chill for several hours.

Serve chilled.

VARIATION

To make Rum Butter, substitute light muscovado sugar for the caster sugar, rum for the brandy and add the finely grated rind of ½ orange.

Brandy Sauce

A soothing, velvety sauce that is excellent with Christmas Pudding (see pages 75 and 76). It can be made in advance and reheated gently, in which case, rub a little piece of butter over the surface to prevent a skin forming while it cools.

SERVES 4–6

50g/2oz butter
50g/2oz plain white flour
600ml/1 pint cold milk
50g/2oz caster sugar
3–4 tbsp brandy
50ml/2fl oz single cream

Melt the butter in a small heavy-based saucepan, mix in the flour, then cook gently for 1 minute, stirring continuously. Gradually add the milk and continue stirring to make a smooth sauce. Add the sugar and simmer the sauce for 2–3 minutes, still stirring continuously, then take the saucepan off the heat and stir in the brandy and cream.

Serve hot with Christmas Pudding (see pages 75 and 76).

Custard Sauce

Real egg custard can be quite pleasing to make, if you are not in a hurry, and is certainly a treat to eat. The only dilemma is how long to cook it and really this is something best judged after a lot of practice. The textbook rule is to dip a cold metal spoon into the custard when you think that it has thickened, then take out the spoon and run your finger along the back of it. If the custard does not drip over the clear part when the spoon is held vertically, the custard is ready. It will thicken a little more as it cools. If the custard is overcooked, it will curdle. A lightly curdled custard can often be saved by plunging the pan (or bowl) into cold water and whisking the custard with a balloon whisk. We have got into the habit of filling the sink with about 25mm/1in of cold water and getting out the balloon whisk before we start, just in case.

SERVES 4–6

600ml/1 pint cold milk
vanilla pod
2 medium eggs
2 medium egg yolks
2 tbsp caster sugar

Put the milk and vanilla pod in a saucepan and bring the milk to boiling point. Remove the pan from the heat, cover with a lid and leave the vanilla pod to infuse for 30 minutes.

Beat the eggs, egg yolks and sugar together, then pour on the warm milk stirring it all together well. Put the custard in the top of a double boiler or use a bowl that fits on top of a saucepan of simmering water, but do not let the bowl touch the water. Stir the custard for about 10 minutes until it has thickened (see above).

To serve warm, pour the custard into a heated jug and stand the jug in a pan of hot, but not boiling, water until needed. To serve cold, pour the custard into a cold jug or bowl and stir as it cools to prevent any skin forming.

Port Wine Sauce

This sauce is a combination of port, orange juice and spices enriched with butter and is adapted from a recipe by Eliza Acton. She suggests serving it with her Christmas Pudding (see page 75).

SERVES 4–6

50g/2oz light muscovado sugar
300ml/½ pint cold water
pared rind of ½ small orange
100g/4oz butter
25g/1oz plain white flour
3 tbsp orange juice
175ml/6fl oz port
freshly grated nutmeg

Put the sugar, water and orange rind in a saucepan and simmer for 10–15 minutes, then strain the syrup.

Melt the butter in a small heavy-based saucepan, stir in the flour, then gradually add the syrup to make a smooth sauce. Simmer the sauce for 2–3 minutes. Add the orange juice, port and some nutmeg.

Serve hot with Eliza Acton's Christmas Pudding (see page 75).

Almond, Hazelnut or Walnut Biscuits

A very simple biscuit recipe. The dough needs to be left in the fridge for several hours before it is used. The biscuits freeze well and defrost quickly, or can be kept in an airtight tin for several days.

MAKES ABOUT 36 BISCUITS
use 2 baking sheets

250g/9oz plain white flour
175g/6oz butter, chilled and cut into pieces, plus a little extra for greasing
75g/3oz caster sugar
100g/4oz walnuts, finely chopped
1 large egg, lightly beaten

Put the flour, butter and sugar into a food processor and process them until the mixture resembles breadcrumbs. Mix in the walnuts briefly. Add the egg and process the dough in short bursts to combine the ingredients. Tip the dough out onto a lightly floured surface and gather it into a smooth ball.

Alternatively, make the dough by rubbing the butter into the flour until the mixture resembles breadcrumbs. Stir in the sugar and walnuts, then mix in the egg and knead the dough until smooth.

Divide the dough in half and make two sausage shapes about 45mm/2in in diameter. Wrap in greaseproof paper and chill for several hours.

Preheat the oven to 190°C/375°F/Gas Mark 5 and lightly butter the baking sheets.

Cut off thin rounds of dough, about 3mm/⅛in thick, and arrange on the baking sheets. Bake the biscuits for about 10–15 minutes until they are golden brown, then transfer to a wire rack to cool completely.

VARIATION

Substitute 100g/4oz finely chopped unblanched almonds *or* 100g/4oz finely chopped roasted hazelnuts for the walnuts.

Macaroons

Macaroons are lovely with ice creams, sorbets, creams and fools and are a good way of using up spare egg whites. Bake them on rice paper, leave them until they are completely cold, then store them in an airtight tin.

MAKES ABOUT 16
use a baking sheet

100g/4oz ground almonds
175g/6oz caster sugar
2 tbsp vanilla sugar (see page 179)
1 tsp plain white flour
2 medium egg whites
about 16 pieces of flaked almond

Preheat the oven to 180°C/350°F/Gas Mark 4 and line a baking sheet with rice paper.

Mix together the ground almonds, sugar, vanilla sugar and flour, then beat in the egg whites. Put teaspoonfuls of the mixture onto the rice paper and press a piece of flaked almond into each macaroon.

Bake the macaroons for 20 minutes, then leave to cool, before tearing away the excess rice paper.

Serve with ice creams, sorbets, creams and fools.

Shortbread

A traditional rich buttery biscuit. Shortbread can be stored in an airtight tin for several days.

MAKES ABOUT 12 PIECES
use a baking sheet

175g/6oz plain white flour
50g/2oz caster sugar
100g/4oz butter, chilled and cut into pieces

Preheat the oven to 180°C/350°F/Gas Mark 4.

Put the flour, sugar and butter into a food processor and process briefly until the mixture resembles breadcrumbs. Alternatively, mix the flour and sugar together and rub in the butter by hand.

Tip the mixture onto a very lightly floured surface, gather it together and knead into a smooth ball of dough. Pat the dough out into a circle about 18cm/7in in diameter and about 5mm/¼in thick.

Put the circle of dough onto the (ungreased) baking sheet, crimp the edge with your thumb, prick it all over with a fork and mark it lightly into sections with the long edge of a spatula or a knife.

Bake the shortbread for 20–25 minutes until it is a very pale golden and just firm to touch. Leave the shortbread to cool a little, then put on a wire rack until completely cold.

Serve with ice creams, sorbets, fruits or fools.

USEFUL NOTES

Ingredients

Milk: We have used semi-skimmed milk in all the recipes, unless whole milk is particularly specified.

Butter: We have used salted butter in all the recipes, unless unsalted butter is particularly specified.

Suet: We have used both shredded beef suet and vegetable suet in our recipes and found them interchangeable.

Eggs: By large eggs we mean size 1 or 2, by medium eggs we mean size 3 and by small eggs we mean size 4 or 5.

Ratafia biscuits: It is important to use ratafias that have apricot kernels among their ingredients as this is what gives them an almond flavour, and some varieties, without kernels, taste rather bland.

Gelatine: In general our measurements have been rounded up or down, but in the case of gelatine we have been more accurate because the powdered gelatine is sold in packs of 11.7g.

Vanilla sugar, rosewater, orange flower water: Vanilla sugar, rosewater and orange flower water can be bought from good delicatessens and some supermarkets.

Rennet: The essential ingredient for a junket. Rennet, lightly sets the milk and is currently available from large branches of good supermarkets. Many wholefood shops sell non-animal rennet which works just as well. Whichever rennet you have, follow the instructions on the bottle. It is critical to have the milk at blood temperature (98.4° C) for the rennet to set the milk and a thermometer is useful, although you can always test the temperature with your finger – the milk should feel warm.

Utensils

Spoons: In all our recipes, a tablespoon measures 15ml, a dessertspoon measures 10ml and a teaspoon measures 5ml.

Pie plate: The plate we use to make plate pies is fairly flat and made in white enamel with a blue rim. We bought it very cheaply in a local hardware store.

Double boiler: We find a stainless steel double boiler invaluable for making curds and custards. It is far more efficient than a basin over a saucepan of water and well worth the investment. Double boilers are available from good kitchen shops and department stores.

Tart tin: We find that a metal tart tin with a removable base is ideal for making tarts, as you can simply press up the base to remove the tart. Also, pastry tends to cook better in a metal tin than in a china flan dish. The tart tins we use are 2.5cm/1in deep, with a fluted edge.

Techniques

Steaming a pudding:

1. Put a trivet or upturned saucer into a large saucepan with a lid. Fill about a quarter of the saucepan with water and bring it to the boil.
2. Fill the pudding basin, leaving enough space at the top for the pudding to rise.
3. Butter a piece of greaseproof paper, make a pleat in it (so that the pudding has room to rise) and cover the pudding. Put a piece of pleated foil over the greaseproof paper and tie them securely under the rim with string (see diagram, right).
4. Trim the greaseproof paper and foil to about 2.5cm/1in away from the string.
5. To make the pudding easier to lift out of the boiling water, make a string handle *or* fold a long strip of foil to go under the basin and up the sides.
6. Put the pudding into the boiling water and check that the water reaches about halfway up the sides of the basin. Put the lid on the saucepan and adjust the heat so that the water is just boiling. Keep checking that there is enough water in the saucepan throughout the cooking time and that the water is at a constant temperature.
7. When the pudding has cooked, take the basin out of the saucepan and leave the pudding to stand for a few minutes. Take off the foil and paper, loosen the edge of the pudding with a knife, put a *deep* plate, upside down, over the pudding basin and turn it over.

Toasting nuts: Put the nuts on a baking tray and grill for a few minutes until they are golden brown, but watch them carefully because they burn very quickly.

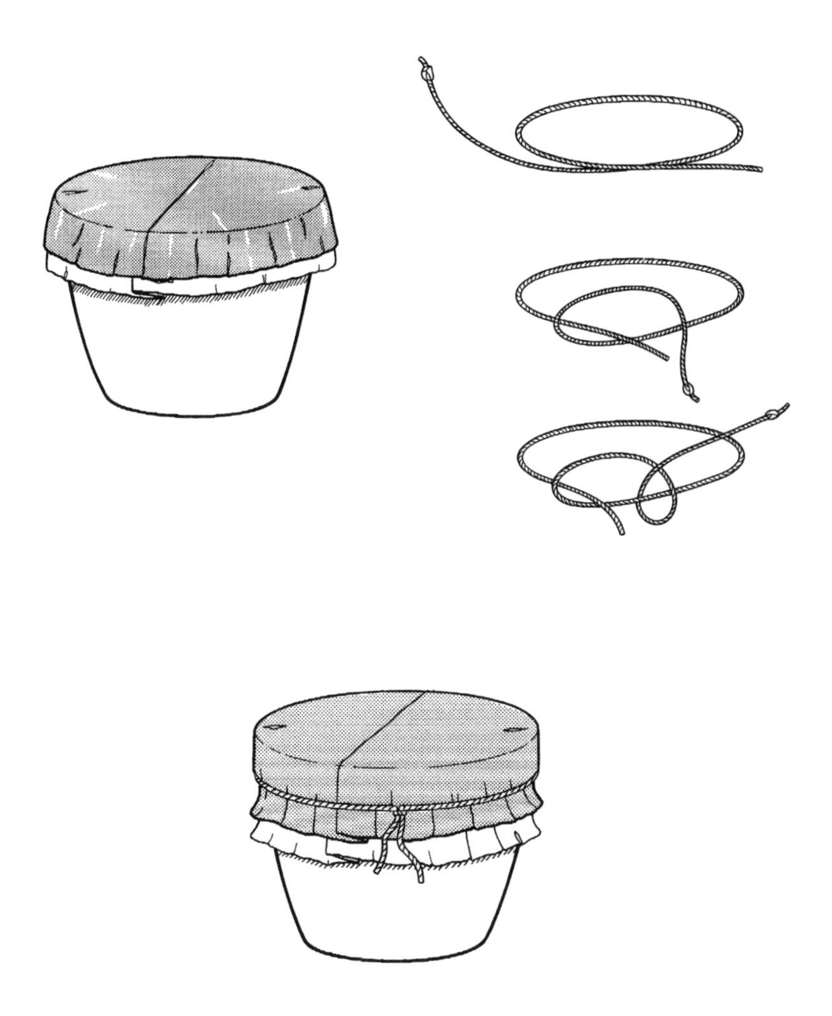

Turning out moulds: A jelly or blancmange is easier to turn out of a mould if it is either *lightly* greased with flavourless cooking oil or wetted with cold water before putting the mixture into it.

Shortcrust pastry: The easiest and most foolproof way to make shortcrust pastry is in a food processor. Process the dry ingredients and the chilled butter, cut into pieces, together until the mixture resembles breadcrumbs. Then add the egg or other liquid and process the mixture as briefly as possible until it forms a smooth dough.

To make shortcrust pastry by hand, cut the chilled butter into pieces and rub it into the flour until the mixture resembles breadcrumbs. Stir in any other dry ingredients. Mix in the egg or other liquid roughly with a knife, then knead into a smooth dough.

Puff pastry: We have used puff pastry in only a couple of recipes because we think that a good, home-made shortcrust is far more practical to prepare and to use. Frozen puff pastry is a handy alternative, but can never be as good as the home-made version, largely because it is made with vegetable oils and not butter.

Lining a tart tin: Roll out the pastry on a cool, lightly floured surface to a circle that is a little larger than the tart tin. Flip the pastry over a rolling pin and lift it into the tin. Press the pastry flat over the base of the tin and well up the sides, then roll the rolling pin all around the top edge of the tin to cut off any excess pastry. (See also, *Utensils*, page 180.)

Lining a pie plate: Follow the instructions given above for lining a tart tin, but trim off the excess pastry with a knife. (See also, *Utensils*, page 179.)

Baking blind: To bake a tart blind, cover the pastry with a piece of greaseproof paper, spread dry or ceramic beans over the base of the tart, then bake as described in the recipe.

EQUIVALENTS FOR U.S. COOKS

Terms

baking sheet – cookie sheet
biscuits – cookies
caster sugar – superfine sugar
double cream – heavy cream
flaked almonds – slivered almonds
frying pan – skillet
greaseproof – waxed
grill – broiler
icing sugar – confectioner's sugar
pie dish – deep ovenproof baking dish with a flat rim
plain flour – all-purpose flour
pudding basin – pudding bowl
rind – peel
self-raising flour – self-rising flour
single cream – light cream
tart tin – tart pan
toasted – broiled
vanilla pod – vanilla bean

Measurements

These weights are equivalent to 1 U.S. cup

breadcrumbs, fresh 50g/2oz
butter 225g/8oz
candied rind (peel) 150–175g/5–6oz
curd cheese 225g/8oz
flour, all purpose 125g/4oz
golden syrup 350g/12oz
jam 225g/8oz
jelly 300g/10oz
macaroni 75g/3oz
marmalade 225g/8oz

porridge oats 225g/8oz
preserved ginger 250g/9oz
ratafia biscuits (cookies), crumbs 120g/4½oz
rice, short grain 200g/7oz
sago 150g/5oz
semolina 175g/6oz
suet, shredded 150g/5oz
sugar, caster (superfine) 225g/8oz
sugar, demerara, packed 225g/8oz
unpacked 150g/5oz
sugar, granulated 200g/7oz
sugar, muscovado/soft brown, packed 225g/8oz
unpacked 150g/5oz
tapioca 150g/5oz
tea leaves 50g/2oz

Nuts

almonds, flaked (slivered) 120g/4½oz
almonds, ground 100g/4oz
almonds, whole 150g/5oz
hazelnuts 135g/4¾oz
pistachio nuts, shelled 150g/5oz
walnuts 120g/4½oz

Fresh fruit

apples, grated 75g/3oz
blackberries 150g/5oz
blackcurrants 120g/4½oz
carrots, chopped 150g/5oz
cherries, pitted 150g/5oz
unpitted 120g/4½oz
damsons, whole, unpitted 150g/5oz
pitted and halved 175g/6oz
gooseberries, topped and tailed 150g/5oz

parsnips, chopped 150g/5oz
plums, whole and unpitted 150g/5oz
pitted and halved 175g/6oz
raspberries 120g/4½oz
redcurrants 120g/4½oz
rhubarb, chopped 120g/4½oz
strawberries, whole berries 150g/5oz

Dried fruits

currants 150g/5oz
pears (uncooked) 175g/6oz
pineapple, chopped 120g/4½oz
prunes, chopped 100g/4oz
raisins, seedless 165g/5½oz
sultanas 175g/6oz

gelatine, powdered 1 envelope = 1 scant tablespoon

LIQUID MEASUREMENTS

English	*American*
1.2 litres/2 pints	2½ pints/5 cups
600ml/1 pint (20fl oz)	1¼ pints/2½ cups
300ml/½ pint (10fl oz)	1¼ cups
150ml/¼pint (5fl oz)	½ cup
50ml/2fl oz	¼ cup

AFTERWORD

Whether anyone living with two women who are writing a book on puddings is to be envied or pitied will rather turn on whether you take a cavalier or roundhead view of life. On the one hand, you will be the first taster on hand to try any number of delicious dishes. On the other, you are evidently exposed to all manner of temptations on top of the usual ones. In this great schism I am an unashamed cavalier.

The last year has been remarkable not so much for the puds as for the sense of taking part in an exhilarating adventure. What this book clearly demonstrates, I submit, is that the revolution in British cooking is gathering speed and clout as it surges forward, with our unsurpassed sweet dishes in the vanguard of the advance. The island race is rediscovering its ancient heritage, that passion for and delight in puddings which François Mission noted 300 years ago. While French desserts are stuck in their traditional mode, changing only visually as their makers sculpt ever more outlandish shapes to embody the same old recipes, British puds are evolving and emerging as clear world leaders – yet another first for which we perversely take no credit.

So this book is not simply about rediscovering lost delights; it is equally in the business of refining and adapting those forgotten pleasures to modern tastes and lifestyles. It makes for sensuous reading: the honey and orange flower water that turns plain custard tart into a show-stopper; the junket delicately flavoured with elderflowers, coffee, or brandy; the lovely fresh golden orange of an apricot sorbet; the ice cream in which redcurrants are scattered like crimson pearls.

Just how much loving work went into this cornucopia of delights is only occasionally glimpsed in a throwaway line: they were surprised to find so many varieties of Black Cap Pudding in old cookery books 'especially as so many of them did not seem to work'. Theirs does. Then they let slip that they struggled desperately to make a meringue that didn't flop for the Snow and Cream recipe. Theirs doesn't. So an awful lot of hard grafting went into sorting out the problem before you start, into giving a new twist and style to a whole gallimaufry of grand old dishes, and making this book a resounding celebration of the best puds in the world.

Godfrey Smith, 1996

BIBLIOGRAPHY

Eliza Acton, *Modern Cookery for Private Families* (1845, reprinted 1993)
Isabella Beeton, *The Book of Household Management* (1861, reprinted many times)
Bernard N. Bessunger, *Recipes of Old England* (1973)
Arabella Boxer, *Book of English Food* (1991)
English Heritage, *A Taste of History* (1993)
John Farley, *The London Art of Cookery* (1789)
Charles Elme Francatelli, *The Royal English and Foreign Confectioner* (1862)
Hannah Glasse, *The Art of Cookery Made Plain and Easy* (1760)
Farmers' Weekly, *Farmhouse Fare Country Recipes* (1935)
Jessie Lindsay and V. H. Mottram, *Manual of Modern Cookery* (1927)
Jane Grigson, *English Food* (1974)
Jane Grigson, *Fruit Book* (1982)
Jane Grigson, *Good Things* (1971)
Dorothy Hartley, *Food in England* (1954)
Margaret Jensen, *Christiana Awdry's Household Book* (1995)
Mrs C. F. Leyel and Miss Olga Hartley, *The Gentle Art of Cookery* (1925)
C. B. Peacock, *The Practical Daily Menu* (1926)
Elizabeth Raffald, *The Experienced English Housekeeper* (1805)
Elizabeth Ray, *Alexis Soyer: Cook Extraordinary* (1991)
Reader's Digest, *The Cookery Year* (1973)
Reader's Digest, *Farmhouse Cookery* (1980)
Eliza Smith, *The Compleat Housewife* (1758)
Alexis Soyer, *A Culinary Campaign* (1991)
Constance Spry and Rosemary Hume, *The Constance Spry Cookery Book* (1956)
Hilary Spurling, *Elinor Fettiplace's Receipt Book* (1604, reprinted 1987)
Katie Stewart, *Katie Stewart's Cookbook* (1983)
J. H. Walsh, *The English Cookery Book* (1858)
Florence White, *Good Things in England* (1932)
Mrs Mabel Wijey, *Warne's Everyday Cookery* (1950s)
D. Williamson, *The Practice of Cookery and Pastry* (1896)

INDEX

ACKNOWLEGEMENTS

We should like to thank our friends and family for testing and tasting the puds with such enthusiasm. Our thanks also to Kate Quarry who saw the book to press for us with great care and patience. Above all, our gratitude goes to our publisher Colin Webb for his endless stream of ideas and continuous encouragement